Welcome to Atkins Best Recipes

The publication you hold in your hands is a first. Although *Dr. Atkin*
Diet Revolution (complete with recipes) is one of the top 50 best-selling books
with more than 15 million copies in print—this is the first time that w
with photographs. We are confident that this premiere edition will be

It is fitting that our focus is on food. The success of any lor
program comes down to offering a wide array of delicious, palate-tem,
dishes. After all, no matter how strong your commitment to slim down, i.   ...ued food
is boring or tasteless or if it leaves you always feeling hungry, it's just
a matter of time before you revert to the way of eating that got
you in trouble in the first place. And therein lies the problem with
most low-fat, low-calorie weight-loss programs: The food—and the
quantity—just isn't satisfying.

When you do Atkins, it is a very different story. You eat filling
portions of delectable foods. Because natural fats such as olive oil,
cream, and butter actually help you lose weight when you control
the amount of carbohydrates you eat, you get to enjoy such
luxurious dishes as Crispy Buttermilk Fried Chicken, Roast Beef
with Horseradish Crust, and Double Chocolate–Pecan Ice Cream.
Secondly, unlike a diet, the Atkins program is not something that you
stop after you've lost pounds. Instead, you move through four
increasingly liberal phases so that by the time you've reached your
goal weight you'll have learned a new and permanent way of
eating. That know-how will allow you to control your weight—once
and for all. Your days of yo-yo dieting will soon be a distant memory!

The recipes that follow should dispel several myths. For example:

- On Atkins you just eat steak and lamb chops. Of the hundred-plus
  main dish recipes, dozens are for poultry, fish, or shellfish. We
  even offer a chapter on vegetarian entrées.

- On Atkins you can't eat vegetables and fruits. The Salads & Sides chapter should put that
  falsehood to bed, once and for all.

- There's nothing to eat for breakfast but bacon and eggs. Wrong again. Check out the
  Breakfast & Brunch chapter for a host of other start-the-day-right treats.

- You can't exercise your sweet tooth on Atkins. See what awaits you in Desserts & Sweets!

The biggest myth of all is that the food you eat when you do Atkins is boring or bland.
The truth is that with the recipes that follow you'll be able to craft a way of eating that suits
your palate as well as your waistline. But before you whip out the skillet and tie on an apron,
take the time to read our brief summary of the four phases of Atkins and the lists of ingredients
that will make doing Atkins even easier.

Note also that each recipe indicates the phases of Atkins for which it is appropriate, the
correct serving size, and nutritional data. Although we provide the grams of fat and calorie
count for those of you used to low-fat programs, the only numbers you need to count are
the Net Carbs. (See page 6 for an explanation of Net Carbs.)

Please send your feedback on our premiere issue to atkinsrecipes@atkins.com. I hope to
incorporate your suggestions into future editions.

page 157

Olivia Bell Buehl
Director of Information
Atkins Health & Medical Information Services

Time Inc. HOME ENTERTAINMENT

President: Rob Gursha
Vice President, Branded Businesses: David Arfine
Vice President, New Product Development: Richard Fraiman
Executive Director, Marketing Services: Carol Pittard
Director, Retail & Special Sales: Tom Mifsud
Director of Finance: Tricia Griffin
Prepress Manager: Emily Rabin
Book Production Manager: Jonathan Polsky
Associate Product Manager: Victoria Alfonso

Special thanks: Bozena Bannett, Alex Bliss, Robert Dente, Gina Di Meglio, Anne-Michelle Gallero, Peter Harper, Suzanne Janso, Robert Marasco, Natalie McCrea, Mary Jane Rigoroso, Steven Sandonato, Grace Sullivan

Published by Time Inc. Home Entertainment
Time Inc. Home Entertainment is a subsidiary of Time Inc.
Time Inc.
1271 Avenue of the Americas
New York, New York 10020

A ROUNDTABLE PRESS BOOK
For Roundtable Press, Inc.:
Directors: Marsha Melnick, Julie Merberg
Project Editor: Sara Newberry
Production Editor: John Glenn
Design: Blue Anchor Design

ATKINS NUTRITIONALS, INC.
Paul D. Wolff: Chairman & CEO
Scott Kabak: President & COO

Atkins Health & Medical Information Services
Senior Vice President: Michael Bernstein
Director of Information: Olivia Bell Buehl
Managing Editor: Christine M. Senft, M.S.
Food Editor: Stephanie Nathanson
Director of Education & Research: Colette Heimowitz, M.S.
Coordinator, Education & Research: Eva Katz, M.P.H., R.D.
Assistant: Kathy Maguire

Recipe Developers: Grady Best, Cynthia DePersio, Philippe Feret, Wendy Kalen, Tracey Seaman
Photography © by Mark Ferri, with the exception of photographs © by Judd Pilossof on pages 25, 38, 41, 54, 57, 63, 74, 84, 108, 152, 159.
Food Stylists: A.J. Battifarano, Michael Pederson, Fred Thompson
Prop Stylists: Francine Matalon-Degni, Tracy Needle

For more information on Atkins, go to www.atkins.com.

CONTENTS

THE SKINNY ON ATKINS

page 63

RECIPES

page 152

CARBOHYDRATE GRAM COUNTER

page 58

The Skinny on Atkins

With delicious foods like salmon, pork, eggs, and cheese getting the thumbs-up on Atkins, there's no doubt it's an appealing way to lose weight, improve your health, and gain more energy. Created by the late Robert C. Atkins, M.D., 40 years ago and successfully followed by millions of people, the four-phase program known as the Atkins Nutritional Approach™ (ANA) is completely unlike those numbingly bland low-fat, low-calorie weight-loss programs so many of us have tried without success. Despite the long-term popularity of Atkins, however, both the government and the medical establishment have traditionally favored the low-fat route. But recently, two issues have challenged this staid thinking about shedding pounds.

First, the swelling epidemic of obesity—65 percent of the American population is now overweight or obese—and the parallel epidemic of Type 2 diabetes, which is closely linked to excess body weight, is proof that our obsession with restricting fat isn't working. Second, a substantial and growing body of research conducted at prestigious universities and medical centers has shown that the controlled carbohydrate dietary approach is actually more effective for weight loss than low-fat plans. Moreover, programs that control carbs have repeatedly shown greater improvement in triglyceride and cholesterol levels than do low-fat programs. The longer-term studies also show that compared with people on low-fat diets, individuals following Atkins, or any controlled carb program, are more likely to stay with their dietary regimen—no surprise, when you consider the food selection—resulting in a far better shot at permanent weight control.

This relatively recent shift has intensified interest in doing Atkins. And now a controlled carb lifestyle can be even easier and more comprehensive, thanks to the people at Atkins Nutritionals, who continue Dr. Atkins' legacy with www.atkins.com and a host of books and other information products, as well as a line of delicious low carb foods.

Why Do Atkins?

There are four reasons to do Atkins. The first two are weight loss and its partner, weight maintenance. The second two are good health and disease prevention. If you're interested in any, or all, of those benefits, keep reading.

Weight Loss

Here's how doing Atkins works: Your body burns both carbohydrate and fat as fuel for its energy needs. It turns first to carbohydrate; however, when you sufficiently cut down on the amount of carbs you eat, your body must instead burn fat—including the fat on your hips, thighs, tummy, or wherever—as its primary energy source. The result: You lose weight.

In fact, almost all men and women who follow the ANA readily take off pounds—and inches. Typically men lose faster than women, and younger people and those who are more active lose more quickly than older folks or couch potatoes. (And by the way, exercise is an integral component of slimming down and toning up on Atkins, as it is with any weight-loss program.)

After kick-starting your weight loss in the Induction phase, you progressively increase your carbohydrate intake until you have added most foods back into your diet. The first key to continuing Atkins is finding your Critical Carbohydrate Level for Losing (CCLL), the grams of Net Carbs that allow you to slowly but consistently lose extra pounds. Optimizing body weight is important, not just for your looks, your energy level, and your self-esteem—it is a crucial component of good health, because being significantly overweight is usually an indicator of health problems, either now or in the future.

Weight Maintenance

Remember, getting to your goal weight is not the grand finale. The real goal is to maintain your weight loss indefinitely. This is where Atkins is so effective and the reason it is deemed a lifestyle, not a diet. Each one of us has a highly individualized level of carbohydrate intake that allows us to neither gain nor lose weight. This is known as your Atkins Carbohydrate Equilibrium™ (ACE) and is the second key to success on Atkins. Understanding how to use this tool allows you to maintain a healthy weight for life.

Good Health and Disease Prevention

When you do Atkins properly, you rely on the carbohydrate sources that are most nutrient-rich—and high in fiber. You are also eating proteins such as fish, poultry, red meat, eggs, and cheese, and natural fats like olive oil and avocado. As a result, you are more likely to meet your nutritional needs and enjoy good health than you would be by following a low-fat, calorie-restricted diet. At its most basic, doing Atkins means you are eating healthy, wholesome foods and omitting bleached flour, sugar, and all processed junk food, which is also typically swimming in artery-damaging trans fats.

When you eat the Atkins way, you will start feeling fabulous well before you reach your goal weight. This is not merely because excess pounds and inches drop off, but because in many cases the consequences of dysfunctional blood sugar and insulin metabolism are reversed. The resulting lowered insulin production means that individuals at high risk for chronic illnesses such as cardiovascular disease, hypertension, and diabetes will see a marked improvement in their risk indicators, like total cholesterol and blood glucose levels. And the rest of us won't become high-risk candidates for disease.

The Four Phases of Atkins

The cornerstone of the Atkins philosophy is a four-phase eating plan combined with vitamin and mineral supplementation and exercise. Following this approach lays the groundwork for a lifetime of good health.

The individualized eating plan allows you to select which foods to eat based on your weight-loss or weight-maintenance goals, as well as your food preferences. Your food selections will differ to varying degrees depending upon the phase you are in and your individual metabolism. The phases in the Atkins roadmap to sustained success are:

Phase 1: Induction

During Induction, you limit carbohydrate consumption to 20 grams of Net Carbs each day. This phase kicks off weight loss. (As with any weight-loss program, most of the initial pounds lost are water.) Carbohydrates should come primarily from salad greens and other non-starchy vegetables. You may consume one slice of low carb bread or one low carb tortilla per day. It is important to understand that the Induction phase is not going to be your lifelong way of eating. It will last a minimum of fourteen days, after which you should see significant results.

Induction is designed to do all of the following for you:

- Switch your body from a carb-burning metabolism to a primarily fat-burning one.
- Stabilize your blood sugar and halt symptoms of unstable blood sugar, such as fatigue, mood swings, and "brain fog."
- Curb your cravings for high carb foods.
- Break addictions to foods such as sugar, wheat, corn, alcohol, or caffeine.
- Demonstrate how much body fat you can burn while enjoying liberal portions of tasty foods.

Phase 2 Recipes:
* Generally contain no more than 10 grams of Net Carbs per serving.
* Can include low carb pasta, all cheeses, and nuts and seeds and their butters.

Phase 3 and 4 Recipes:
* May include ingredients restricted in earlier phases.

Note: Depending upon your metabolism and tolerance for certain carbohydrate foods, you may or may not necessarily be able to eat all dishes coded for the phase you are in. Or if you have a high metabolism, you may be able to eat meals coded for Phases 3 and 4 while you are still in OWL. Remember that you still must count your daily intake of Net Carbs.

What Are Net Carbs?

When you do Atkins, you actually count only Net Carbs—the total carbohydrate content of the food minus the fiber content (along with glycerine and sugar alcohols found in some low carb foods). Net Carbs reflect the grams of carbohydrate that significantly impact your blood sugar level and are the only carbs you need to count when you do Atkins. The Net Carb number is almost always lower than the total carbohydrate number. The exception is foods such as cream with virtually no fiber content. In such cases the total carbs and Net Carbs are identical.

In the second phase, you deliberately slow your weight loss by progressively increasing your carbohydrate intake. You do this by continuing to eat nutrient-dense and fiber-rich foods, although you now have more choices. The first week you increase to 25 daily grams of Net Carbs, go to 30 grams daily the next week, and so on until weight loss stops. At that point drop back 5 grams daily and you will have found your Critical Carbohydrate Level for Losing (CCLL), which should allow you to continue sustained, moderate weight loss. Induction takes weight off quickly, but OWL lets you personalize the ANA to your tastes and needs.

On OWL you will:

- Continue to burn fat.
- Maintain control of your appetite sufficiently to manage cravings.
- Learn your CCLL, which will allow you to continue to lose weight.
- Eat a broader range of healthy foods, selecting those you enjoy most.
- Learn to make the most nutrient-rich choices among carbohydrate foods such as seeds and nuts, berries, and other low-glycemic fruits. A few people can even gradually introduce small portions of whole grains, legumes, fruits other than berries, or starchy vegetables.
- Deliberately slow your rate of weight loss to lay the groundwork for permanent weight management.

Phase 3: Pre-Maintenance

Move to the third phase of the ANA, which bridges weight loss and weight maintenance, when you're within five to ten pounds of your goal. You can now increase your daily Net Carb intake in weekly increments of 10 grams so long as almost imperceptible weight loss continues. In Pre-Maintenance, if you are like most people, you can gradually add back legumes, whole grains, fruits (in addition to berries), and even an occasional starchy vegetable. Portions should be small, and most of these foods should be eaten only occasionally.

When it comes to the last few pounds, slower is better. That way, by the time you reach your goal weight you will know exactly how you will be eating for the rest of your life—and controlling your carb intake should have become automatic. By the time you have reached and maintained your goal weight for at least a month, you should know your ACE and will have officially transitioned to Lifetime Maintenance.

During Pre-Maintenance you will:

- Find your new CCLL and ultimately your ACE.
- Explore more food choices, while learning not to abuse them, adding new foods one at a time. Eliminate a new food if it provokes weight gain, any symptoms lost during Induction, increased appetite, cravings, or water retention.
- Become aware of the foods or situations that can make you lose sight of your long-term goals.
- Internalize your responses to food so that what used to be a struggle becomes a conscious choice.
- Find out how flexible Atkins is.
- Learn how to deal with temptation.
- Discover how to immediately erase the problems created by making unhealthy food choices.
- Practice the style of eating you will follow for a lifetime.

Phase 4: Lifetime Maintenance

In this last phase, you continue to select from a wide variety of foods while controlling carbohydrate intake to ensure weight maintenance and a sense of well-being. This lifestyle is the foundation for a lifetime of better health. You also must conquer your former bad habits and learn how to handle real-world challenges. For example, you'll need coping strategies for holidays and other special occasions, as well as for dining out.

Adhering to Lifetime Maintenance will:

- Provide you with a way of eating that allows you to stay slim for the rest of your life.
- Allow you to maximize the amount of healthy carbohydrate foods you can eat while staying within three to five pounds of your goal weight.
- Prevent re-addiction to certain foods by helping you avoid frequent exposure.
- Teach you how to drop back to an earlier weight-loss phase, when necessary, to trim off a few pounds.
- Show you how to adjust your carbohydrate consumption when metabolic circumstances change—for example, when your activity level is temporarily decreased because of a sports injury—before you find yourself regaining inches and/or weight.
- Reduce your risk factors for cardiovascular disease, hypertension, diabetes, and other sugar-metabolism disorders.
- Give you a sense of accomplishment and confidence that spills over into the rest of your life.

For more on the four phases of Atkins and the science behind Atkins, go to www.atkins.com. Also read *Dr. Atkins' New Diet Revolution* (Avon), *Atkins for Life* (St. Martin's), and *The Atkins Essentials* (Avon).

Acceptable Foods

There are two main reasons for the four phases of Atkins. First you reduce your carb intake to 20 grams of Net Carbs a day to kick-start weight loss in Induction. In that phase, your carbs come primarily from salad greens and other low-glycemic vegetables. Second, as you proceed through the phases you gradually increase both the variety and amount of other nutrient-dense carbohydrate foods. By the time you reach Lifetime Maintenance, you should have reintroduced almost all carbohydrate foods—although not everyone is able to do so—with the exception of sugar and bleached flour, and the highly processed foods made with them. (That is not to say that on special occasions you will not be able to make an exception to this rule as long as you do not use it as an excuse to fall back into old bad habits.)

It is important to understand that not everyone can reintroduce foods such as fruit, legumes, whole grains, and starchy vegetables like sweet potatoes without regaining weight. Factors such as gender, age, activity level, hormonal status, and even genetics play a role in your metabolism, which influences how high your ACE will be in Lifetime Maintenance. If you are someone with an ACE of, say, 40, you will be unlikely to be eating brown rice—a half cup contains almost 21 grams of Net Carbs—very often. Likewise, a half-cup of pinto beans delivers almost 15 grams of Net Carbs.

How to Calculate Net Carbs

You can guesstimate the grams of Net Carbs for a particular food by using the information provided by the Nutrition Facts panel on the label. Simply subtract the grams of fiber from the grams of total carbs per serving and you've got a pretty good sense of the Net Carb number. For fresh foods and other unpackaged foods, you'll need to refer to a carb gram counter (see inside). For a complete carb gram counter, see *Dr. Atkins' New Carbohydrate Gram Counter* (M. Evans).

Acceptable Induction Foods

PROTEINS AND FATS

You can eat liberal amounts of the following foods. Eat only until you are full but not stuffed.

Meat:

Beef	Pork/Ham/Bacon	Veal
Lamb	Rabbit	Venison

Note: Do not consume more than 4 ounces of organ meats a day. Processed meats such as bacon, ham, pepperoni, salami, hot dogs, and other luncheon meats may be cured with added sugar, and may contain nitrates. Also avoid products that are not exclusively meat, such as meatloaf or breaded foods.

Poultry:

Chicken	Duck	Pheasant	Turkey
Cornish hen	Goose	Quail	Other game birds

Note: Avoid breaded chicken breasts and other poultry products that are not exclusively meat.

Fish (including canned):

Anchovies	Cod	Mahi-mahi	Salmon	Swordfish
Bass	Flounder	Monkfish	Sardines	Trout
Bluefish	Herring	Orange roughy	Scrod	Tuna
Catfish	Mackerel	Red snapper	Sole	Whitefish

Note: Avoid fish cured with sugar or nitrates.

Shellfish:

Clams	Lobster	Oysters	Shrimp
Crab	Mussels	Scallops	Squid
Crawfish	Octopus		

Note: Oysters and mussels are higher in carbs than other shellfish, so limit them to 4 ounces a day. Avoid imitation shrimp or crab, which are made with high carb fillers.

Eggs and Cheese:

Eggs, prepared any style

You may eat up to 4 ounces of full-fat, firm, soft, and semi-soft aged cheeses such as:

Asiago	Cheddar	Goat cheese	Jarlsberg	Parmesan
Blue cheese	Cream cheese	Gouda	Monterey Jack	Parmigiano
Brie	Feta	Gruyère	Mozzarella	Provolone
Camembert	Fontina	Havarti	Muenster	Swiss

Note: All cheeses have some carbohydrate content, which governs quantities. The rule of thumb is to count 1 ounce of cheese as 1 gram of carbohydrate. Fresh cheese, such as cottage cheese, ricotta, and farmer cheese, is too high in carbs for Induction. Avoid diet cheeses or cheese spreads. Individuals with a known yeast intolerance, dairy allergy, or milk intolerance must avoid cheese. Imitation cheese products are not allowed except for soy or rice cheese—but always check the carb content.

Soy:

Tofu (bean curd)

Fats and Oils:

Butter	Sour cream	Canola oil	Safflower oil
Cream	Whipped cream	Corn oil	Sesame oil
Half-and-half	(unsweetened)	Flaxseed oil	Soybean oil
Mayonnaise		Grapeseed oil	Sunflower oil
		Olive oil	Walnut oil

Note: Oils labeled "cold-pressed" or "expeller-pressed" have the most nutrients. Avoid margarine, which is usually made with hydrogenated oils, or trans fats. (Some non-hydrogenated margarines are available in natural food stores and selected supermarkets.)

CARBOHYDRATES

Salad Vegetables: You can have 3 cups (loosely packed) of the following:

Alfalfa sprouts	Chicory	Endive	Mesclun	Radishes
Arugula	Chinese	Escarole	Mushrooms	Romaine
Bean sprouts	cabbage	Fennel	Parsley	Sorrel
Cabbage	Cucumber	Jicama	Peppers	Watercress
Celery	Daikon	Lettuce	Radicchio	

Note: For salad dressing, use oil plus vinegar or lemon juice and spices. You can also use bottled brands of salad dressings with less than 2 grams of Net Carbs per serving.

Other Vegetables: A cup of one of these low carb vegetables can replace a cup of salad.

Artichoke	Broccoli rabe	Green beans	Pumpkin	Tomato
hearts	Brussels	Green onions	Rhubarb	Turnip greens
Asparagus	sprouts	Hearts of palm	Snow peas	Turnips
Avocado	Cauliflower	Kale	Spaghetti	Water
Bamboo	Celery root	Kohlrabi	squash	chestnuts
shoots	Collard greens	Leeks	Spinach	Wax beans
Beet greens	Dandelion	Mustard	Summer	Zucchini
Bok choy	greens	greens	squash	
Broccoli	Eggplant	Okra	Swiss chard	

OTHER FOODS

Herbs and Spices: Season foods, to taste, with any of the following:

Basil	Cilantro	Ginger	Rosemary
Cayenne pepper	Cumin	Oregano	Sage
Chili powder	Dill	Paprika	Tarragon
Chives	Garlic	Pepper	Thyme

Note: Dry granulated spices are allowed as long as they do not contain sugar. If the package mentions additional unspecified "spices," those "spices" may contain sugar.

Salad Garnishes:

Chopped onion	Grated cheese	Minced sautéed	Olives
Crumbled bacon	Minced hardboiled	mushrooms	Sour cream
	egg yolk		

Beverages:

Water	Essence-flavored	Decaffeinated	Clear broth/
Spring water	seltzer (must say	coffee or tea	bouillon
Mineral water	"no calories")	Herb teas	
Club soda	Iced tea		

Note: Herb teas should contain no barley, dates, figs, or sugar. Iced tea can be unsweetened or artificially sweetened. Grain beverages (i.e., imitation coffee substitutes) are not allowed. Alcoholic beverages are not part of Induction, but those low in carbohydrates are, in moderation, an option for the later phases of the program. However, wine can be used in cooking because the alcohol burns off.

Artificial Sweeteners:

Consumed in moderation, artificial sweeteners make it possible for those trying to lose weight to enjoy the taste of sweets.

Sucralose (Splenda®), the only sweetener made from sugar, does not raise blood sugar. The Food and Drug Administration (FDA) approved it in 1998 after reviewing more than 100 studies. Saccharin (Sweet 'N' Low®), cyclamate (Sugar Twin®), and acesulfame-K (Sunett®) are all acceptable as well. Remember each packet of sugar substitute contains about 1 gram of carbohydrate, which must be counted. Consume no more than three a day.

Acceptable OWL Foods

In the second phase of Atkins, most people can reintroduce the following foods:

Nuts, Seeds, and Their Butters:

Almonds	Hazelnuts (filberts)	Pine nuts	Sesame seeds
Brazil nuts	Macadamias	Pistachios	Sunflower seeds
Coconut	Pecans	Pumpkin seeds	Walnuts

Note: If you stay on Induction more than two weeks, you can add nuts and seeds back into your daily total of 20 grams of Net Carbs.

Fresh Cheeses:

Cottage	Goat	Pot
Farmer	Mascarpone	Ricotta

Berries:

Blackberries	Cranberries	Strawberries
Blueberries	Raspberries	

Acceptable Pre-Maintenance Foods

In this phase, most people can add back the following foods. Be sure to introduce only one new food at a time.

Dairy:
Whole milk*
Whole-milk plain yogurt*

Nuts, Seeds, and Their Butters:
Cashews* (Cashew nuts are technically a fruit and are higher in carbs than other nuts.)
Chestnuts**
Peanuts* (Peanuts are technically legumes and also higher in carbs than other nuts.)

Legumes:

Black beans	Kidney beans	Peas, dried/split	Pinto beans*
Black-eyed peas*	Lentils	Pink beans	Soybeans, dried
Chickpeas	Navy beans		

Fruit Other Than Berries:

Apple	Grapefruit	Melon*	Peach	Prunes**
Apricot*	Grapes*	Nectarine*	Pear	Raisins**
Banana**	Kiwi	Orange	Pineapple*	Tangerine
Cherries	Mango*	Papaya*	Plum	Watermelon*

Juices:
Grapefruit juice*
Tomato juice*

Starchy Vegetables:

Beets*	Parsnips**	Pumpkin*	Taro*	Yams*
Carrots*	Peas, green*	Sweet potato**	Winter	Yuca*
Corn, sweet**	Potato, white**		squash*	

Whole Grains:

Amaranth*	Bread, whole	Buckwheat*	Cornmeal**
Barley	wheat	Bulgur*	Oatmeal
Bread, whole	Brown rice	Cereals, whole	Wild rice
grain*		grain**	

*Eat in moderation.
**Eat sparingly.

Keys to the Atkins Kitchen

Without the proper foods at the ready, your weight-loss endeavor can be more difficult—sometimes, even impossible. On the other hand, having a properly stocked kitchen goes a long way toward your success doing Atkins, so plan your shopping expeditions around the following items:

For the Refrigerator

Most of these items have a brief shelf life, so buy them in appropriate quantities to prevent waste. Keep ingredients for easy-to-prepare snacks such as hard-boiled eggs, cheese cubes, cut-up veggies, and creamy dips to grab when hunger strikes. Being prepared is a huge edge when it comes to staying on track.

PROTEIN:
You'll want lots of variety, so have on hand poultry (use within two days of buying or freeze); fish (use the same day you buy or freeze); shellfish (use the same day you buy); and meat (try to buy and use on the same day or freeze); and cold cuts, such as sliced roast beef, turkey breast, and ham. Firm tofu is ideal for stir-fries; silken tofu, for high-protein smoothies.

CHEESE:
Try to keep several varieties in your refrigerator to suit a range of needs: cheddar for burgers, crumbled blue for tossed salads, grated Monterey Jack for omelets, and tasty hard cheeses, such as Parmesan, for snacking.
- Semi-soft cheeses (Brie, Camembert)
- Firmer cheeses (Gruyère, Parmesan, Gouda, cheddar)
- Blue cheeses (Roquefort, Gorgonzola, Maytag Blue)
- Fresh cheeses (cottage cheese, ricotta, goat cheese, mascarpone)

Note: Do not eat fresh cheeses in Induction.

OTHER DAIRY PRODUCTS:
Cream, sour cream, butter, and eggs are all fine in Induction. In later phases, small portions of whole-milk (full-fat) plain yogurt and whole milk are acceptable.

SALAD VEGETABLES:
All are good sources of phytonutrients and fiber. Select from the list on the previous pages.

OTHER VEGETABLES:
Refer to the lists on previous pages and rely on seasonal varieties for best quality and price.

HERBS AND OTHER SEASONINGS:
Fresh herbs make every dish tastier. To keep them fresher longer, wrap them in damp paper towels and store in a plastic bag. Good basics include basil, cilantro, chives, parsley, and dill. Keep a small supply of shallots on hand, as well as celery and fresh ginger. Fresh garlic belongs in every kitchen.

FRUIT:
Lemons and limes add zip to main dishes and salad dressings and can be used in Induction. Once you are in OWL, strawberries, raspberries, blackberries, and blueberries can be whirled into low carb shakes, sprinkled over low carb cereal, or served with whipped cream for dessert. Kiwi, small apricots, rhubarb, and plums are also relatively low in carbs. As you move into Pre-Maintenance, you can probably eat small portions of most fruits. Juice is missing fiber

and is therefore higher in carbs than the equivalent fruit (grapefruit juice is an exception to this rule). Bananas, raisins, and prunes all have high sugar content and should be eaten rarely.

For the Freezer

In addition to keeping a good supply of protein foods, vegetables, and appropriate fruits in your freezer, keep low carb sliced bread there as well, to encourage portion control.

VEGETABLES:

Frozen vegetables are a convenient alternative when fresh varieties are not available—and they're equally nutritious (freshly picked from your garden is ideal!). Some vegetables freeze better than others. A good selection of frozen vegetables would include spinach (both whole leaf and chopped), collard greens, kale, snow peas, green beans, artichoke hearts, asparagus spears, broccoli florets, and cauliflower florets.

FRUIT:

Useful when you have reached OWL are unsweetened strawberries, blueberries, raspberries, and blackberries, as well as rhubarb.

PROTEIN:

For quick meals when you don't have time to shop, keep frozen cooked shrimp and crabmeat (not artificial "crab legs") in the freezer.

NUTS AND SEEDS:

Store macadamia nuts, almonds, walnuts, hazelnuts, pecans, sunflower seeds, and pumpkin seeds in the freezer to keep them from going rancid.

In the Pantry

You'll appreciate having these shelf-stable staples in your cupboards as a backup for times when fresh foods aren't available. Keep a good supply of condiments on hand—they add pizzazz to any dish; together with canned protein, vegetables, and low carb pasta (and whole grains, for later phases), a myriad of meals is yours for the making.

CONDIMENTS:
- Anchovies (in cans or jars)
- Basil pesto (in containers or tubes)
- Capers
- Chiles (in cans)
- Chipotle en adobo (smoked jalapeños in a tomato-vinegar sauce)
- Curry paste
- Horseradish (white)
- Mustard (country-style or Dijon)
- Olive paste
- Porcini mushrooms (dried)
- Soy sauce (reduced-sodium and regular)
- Sugar-free barbecue sauce
- Sugar-free ketchup
- Sun-dried tomatoes (in oil)
- Tabasco® sauce and hot pepper sauce
- Tomato paste (in tubes)
- Vinegars (white wine, red wine, tarragon, rice wine, balsamic)
- Worcestershire sauce

Note: Balsamic vinegar in portions of 1 teaspoon or less is allowed, even on Induction, for cooking.

STAPLES:

- Beef, chicken, and vegetable broths (reduced-sodium)
- Brown rice*
- Bulgur*
- Cornmeal
- Low carb pasta*
- Low carb tortillas
- Oatmeal (old-fashioned style)*
- Pumpkin purée (unsweetened)
- Tomato sauce and chopped tomatoes
- Whole-wheat flour*
- Wild rice*

CANNED PROTEIN AND VEGETABLES:

- Artichoke hearts in marinade
- Beans*
- Nut butters (unsweetened and non-hydrogenated)**
- Roasted red peppers
- Salmon
- Sardines
- Tuna (in olive oil and water)
- White-meat chicken

BAKING BASICS AND SWEET ITEMS:

With low carb wheat-flour substitutes, sweeteners, and flavorings, you can prepare homemade baked goods, desserts, and sugar-free treats.

- Cocoa powder
- Extracts (vanilla, chocolate, banana, hazelnut, almond, coconut)
- Low carb sugar-free pancake syrup
- Low carb bake mixes
- Sugar substitutes (granular form for baking; packets for beverages)
- No-sugar-added jams (OWL and beyond)
- ThickenThin™ Not Starch thickener (for custards, puddings, and thickening soups and stews; available at www.atkins.com)
- Unsweetened baking chocolate

*For later phases only
**For use after the first two weeks of Induction.

Atkins Nutritionals Products

Atkins Nutritionals, Inc., makes a full line of low carbohydrate alternative foods and ingredients, including Atkins Advantage™ Bars and Ready-to-Drink Shakes.

Here are ingredients you will find useful to have in your pantry:

- Atkins Advantage™ Shake Mix in Strawberry, Chocolate, Vanilla, and Cappuccino
- Atkins Quick Quisine™ Bake Mix*
- Atkins Quick Quisine™ Pancake & Waffle Mix*
- Atkins Quick Quisine™ Lemon Poppy Muffin & Bread Mix
- Atkins Quick Quisine™ Orange Cranberry Muffin & Bread Mix
- Atkins Quick Quisine™ Banana Nut Muffin & Bread Mix
- Atkins Quick Quisine™ Chocolate Chocolate Chip Muffin & Bread Mix
- Atkins Kitchen™ Quick & Easy Bread Mix in Country White, Sourdough, and Caraway Rye
- Atkins Bakery™ Ready-to-Eat Sliced Bread* in White, Rye, and Multigrain
- Atkins Bakery™ Freeze N' Thaw Bread
- Atkins Quick Quisine™ Sugar Free Pancake Syrup*
- Atkins™ Sugar Free Syrup in Caramel, Raspberry, Chocolate, and Strawberry
- Atkins Quick Quisine™ Ketch-A-Tomato
- Atkins Quick Quisine™ Barbeque Sauce
- Atkins Quick Quisine™ Steak Sauce*
- Atkins Quick Quisine™ Teriyaki Sauce*
- Atkins Quick Quisine™ Pasta Cuts in Penne, Fusilli, Spaghetti, and Cut Fettuccine*
- Atkins Endulge™ Chocolate Candy Bars*
- Atkins Endulge™ Ice Cream*

*Used in recipes in this book.

All these products can be ordered from www.atkins.com. For local retailers, go to the Store Locator on the Web site or call 1-800-2-ATKINS.

Portabello and Ricotta Crostini, page 18

APPETIZERS & SNACKS

Creamy dips, crunchy crisps, lip-smacking good wings: No wonder finger foods and snacks are so popular. Look no further for savory low carb meal starters or hunger-appeasing snacks that are also a hit with your waistline—the tasty choices abound.

PORTABELLO AND RICOTTA CROSTINI

PER SERVING
Net Carbs: 5.5 grams
Total Carbs: 10 grams
Fiber: 4.5 grams

Protein: 9 grams
Fat: 7 grams
Calories: 136

Servings: 4
Prep time: 15 minutes
Bake/cook time: 30 minutes

Both the toasts (crostini) and topping can be prepared up to a day ahead. If necessary, re-crisp the toasts by baking for a few minutes in a 350° F oven. Tomato pesto in tubes is available in the tomato sauce section of most supermarkets.

1 tablespoon extra-virgin olive oil, divided

½ tablespoon balsamic vinegar

1 large garlic clove, pushed through a press

1 large portabello mushroom, stem and gills removed

4 slices Atkins Bakery™ Ready-to-Eat Sliced White Bread

3 tablespoons ricotta cheese, drained on a doubled paper towel 5 minutes

¼ teaspoon salt

4 teaspoons tomato pesto

Finely chopped fresh parsley, if desired

1 Heat oven to 425° F. Combine half the oil with the vinegar and garlic. Brush mixture on both sides of mushroom. Place mushroom, top side up, on a foil-lined baking sheet. Bake 15 to 18 minutes, until golden. Remove from oven, wrap in foil, and let stand 5 to 8 minutes to soften. Pat mushroom dry with paper towel. Cut in half, then thinly slice crosswise to form crescent-shaped pieces.

2 Meanwhile, heat broiler. Cut two circles from each slice of bread with a 2-inch round biscuit cutter. Brush both sides of circles with remaining oil. Broil on a baking sheet 4 inches from heat source 30 to 40 seconds per side. Transfer toasts to a rack to cool.

3 To assemble: Mix ricotta with salt in a cup. Spread each toast evenly with tomato pesto, then with ricotta. Top with slightly overlapping mushroom slices. Sprinkle with parsley, if desired.

Atkins Tip: Use leftover crusts to make fresh breadcrumbs.

CREAMY CRAB DIP

PER SERVING
Net Carbs: 1 gram
Total Carbs: 1 gram
Fiber: 0 grams

Protein: 6.5 grams
Fat: 9.5 grams
Calories: 115

Servings: 6
Prep time: 10 minutes

Ready in minutes, this crowd-pleasing dip lends itself to variations: Add chopped jalapeño for spiciness or celery for extra crunch. Scoop up dip with endive leaves or serve with low carb bread, toasted and cut into triangles.

¼ cup mayonnaise

¼ cup sour cream

1 teaspoon Old Bay® seasoning

1 teaspoon fresh lemon juice

1 (6-ounce) can white crabmeat, drained and picked over

2 green onions, finely chopped

2 tablespoons chopped red bell pepper

Salt

Freshly ground pepper

1 In a medium bowl, mix mayonnaise, sour cream, seasoning, and lemon juice until smooth.

2 Add crabmeat, green onions, and bell pepper; stir until ingredients are well combined. Season to taste with salt and pepper.

Atkins Tip: You may substitute canned salmon or sardines for the crab.

SPINACH-ARTICHOKE DIP

PER SERVING
Net Carbs: 5 grams
Total Carbs: 7.5 grams
Fiber: 2.5 grams

Protein: 9 grams
Fat: 13 grams
Calories: 177

Servings: 8
Prep time: 5 minutes
Bake/cook time: 30 minutes

Canned artichoke bottoms are called for in this recipe because they have a deeper flavor than frozen artichoke hearts (which, however, can be used in a pinch). This recipe yields four cups and can be kept refrigerated for up to five days.

1 (10-ounce) package frozen chopped spinach, thawed

1 (13.75-ounce) can artichoke bottoms

2 cloves garlic

8 ounces cream cheese

1 cup grated Parmesan cheese

¼ teaspoon pepper

1 Heat oven to 350° F. Grease a 1-quart ovenproof pan. In a food processor, process spinach, artichokes, garlic, cream cheese, Parmesan, and pepper until well combined. Scrape down sides of processor, as needed.

2 Spread spinach mixture in prepared pan. Bake until warmed through, about 30 minutes. Serve hot with cut-up vegetables.

SPICY CALAMARI

PER SERVING

Net Carbs: 10 grams	Protein: 19.5 grams	Servings: 4
Total Carbs: 12 grams	Fat: 8.5 grams	Prep time: 10 minutes
Fiber: 2 grams	Calories: 202	Cook time: 25 minutes

The calamari becomes tender and very flavorful as it cooks in a spicy homemade tomato sauce. This simple dish is a perfect way to start off an Italian meal.

1 pound squid (calamari)

2 tablespoons olive oil

2 large garlic cloves, sliced

½ teaspoon red pepper flakes

1 (14½-ounce) can diced tomatoes

1 teaspoon dried basil leaves

½ teaspoon dried oregano

Dash sugar substitute

Salt

Freshly ground pepper

1 Clean squid under running water. Remove and discard hard clear pieces in centers. Cut squid into ½-inch rings; halve tentacles.

2 In a medium saucepan over medium heat, cook olive oil, garlic, and red pepper flakes 1 to 2 minutes or until garlic is lightly golden. Remove garlic with a slotted spoon and reserve.

3 Add tomatoes, basil, oregano, and sugar substitue to saucepan. Bring to boil; add squid. Reduce heat to low and cook 20 to 25 minutes or until squid is tender, stirring occasionally. Season to taste with salt and pepper. Transfer to a serving dish and scatter reserved garlic over the top.

SMOKED PROVOLONE–CAPONATA SQUARES

PER SERVING

Net Carbs: 3 grams	Protein: 7 grams	Servings: 4
Total Carbs: 6 grams	Fat: 6.5 grams	Prep time: 10 minutes
Fiber: 3 grams	Calories: 110	Cook time: 5 minutes

Jarred caponata—an Italian eggplant appetizer found in supermarkets—makes a great base for this easy hors d'oeuvre.

2 slices Atkins Bakery™ Ready-to-Eat Sliced White Bread, toasted

½ cup prepared caponata

2 ounces smoked Provolone cheese, grated

Freshly ground pepper

1 Heat broiler. Lay bread on a work surface and evenly spread slices with caponata. Cut each slice into 4 pieces. Sprinkle with cheese and pepper.

2 Broil 30 seconds, until cheese starts to melt. Serve immediately.

BUFFALO CHICKEN WINGS

PER SERVING

Net Carbs: 5.5 grams
Total Carbs: 6 grams
Fiber: 0.5 grams

Protein: 19 grams
Fat: 65 grams
Calories: 678

Servings: 6
Prep time: 25 minutes
Bake/cook time: 20 minutes

Finger food at its best! Whip up a batch of these crispy hot wings for a sure-fire crowd pleaser. Serve with celery sticks and our creamy blue cheese sauce (below).

1 egg

½ cup canola oil

1 cup cider vinegar

1 teaspoon salt

½ teaspoon pepper

Cayenne pepper, to taste

½ teaspoon garlic powder

½ teaspoon celery salt

2 pounds chicken wings

BLUE CHEESE DUNKING SAUCE:

1 cup mayonnaise

½ cup sour cream

1 green onion, chopped

1 garlic clove, pushed through a press

1 tablespoon lemon juice

¼ cup crumbled blue cheese

1 FOR MARINADE: Heat oven to 450° F. Beat egg in a medium bowl. Add oil and beat until combined. Add vinegar, salt, pepper, cayenne, garlic powder, and celery salt; stir until well combined.

2 Cut chicken wings in half at joint; remove wing tips and discard. Dip chicken pieces into marinade and arrange on a large baking pan.

3 Bake 20 minutes, turning and brushing with marinade several times, until wings are crisp. Remove from oven; drain and arrange on a warm platter. Serve with Blue Cheese Dunking Sauce.

4 FOR DUNKING SAUCE: Combine all ingredients. Mix well.

SHRIMP COCKTAIL WITH TWO SAUCES

PER SERVING
Net Carbs: 1.5 grams
Total Carbs: 1.5 grams
Fiber: 0 grams

Protein: 6 grams
Fat: 4 grams
Calories: 65

Servings: 6
Prep time: 20 minutes
Cook time: 5 minutes

Red and green cocktail sauces make this appetizer both festive and tasty. One is spicy, the other mild.

24 large or jumbo shrimp

2 tablespoons red horseradish sauce

1 tablespoon mayonnaise

½ red bell pepper, coarsely chopped

½ teaspoon Worcestershire sauce

2 tablespoons sugar-free green salsa

¼ cup parsley leaves, stems removed

1 green onion, coarsely chopped

2 teaspoons olive oil

1 tablespoon chopped chives or finely chopped green end of a green onion

1 Bring a large pot of lightly salted water to a boil. Peel shrimp (leave tails on, if desired). Remove black veins from each shrimp with a small sharp knife; rinse shrimp.

2 Cook shrimp 3 to 5 minutes just until opaque and cooked through. Remove with a slotted spoon and refresh under cold water (shrimp may be made 1 day ahead).

3 In a food processor or blender, process horseradish, mayonnaise, pepper, and Worcestershire sauce until fairly smooth. Transfer to a bowl; clean bowl of food processor.

4 Process salsa, parsley, onion, and oil until fairly smooth. On each serving plate, place 1 tablespoon red sauce and 1 tablespoon green sauce side by side. Spread sauces out toward the edge of the plate with the tip of a knife. Arrange 4 shrimp in a circular pattern over sauce. Sprinkle with chopped chives.

SMOKED SALMON ROLL-UPS

PER SERVING
Net Carbs: 4 grams
Total Carbs: 13 grams
Fiber: 9 grams

Protein: 15 grams
Fat: 14 grams
Calories: 210

Servings: 4
Prep time: 15 minutes

Fresh vegetable cream cheese and smoky salmon are even more delicious when rolled in low carb tortillas.

4 ounces cream cheese

2 green onions, finely chopped

1 tablespoon chopped fresh dill

4 green onion–flavored low carb tortillas

6 ounces smoked salmon, thinly sliced

1 In a bowl, mix cream cheese, onions, and dill. Spread mixture evenly over tortillas.

2 Layer salmon over cream cheese. Roll up tortillas. Cut each tortilla into 4 pieces.

SPICY OLIVES

PER SERVING
Net Carbs: 1.5 grams
Total Carbs: 2.5 grams
Fiber: 1 gram

Protein: 0.5 grams
Fat: 7 grams
Calories: 70

Servings: 8
Prep time: 5 minutes

A few additions from your spice rack turn plain olives into addictive little nibbles. These are ideal paired with Old Amsterdam cheese (aged Gouda), cut into cubes.

2 cups oil-cured black olives

3 tablespoons olive oil

½ teaspoon crumbled dried rosemary

½ teaspoon red pepper flakes

½ teaspoon dried thyme

½ teaspoon coarsely ground pepper

1 Mix all ingredients in a bowl.

2 Transfer to a jar and let marinate 1 hour. Olives may be kept refrigerated for up to a week. Before serving, bring to room temperature.

ATKINS GARLIC TOAST CRISPS

PER SERVING
Net Carbs: 2 grams
Total Carbs: 3 grams
Fiber: 1 gram

Protein: 1.5 grams
Fat: 3.5 grams
Calories: 70

Servings: 20
Prep time: 10 minutes
Bake time: 1 hour 15 minutes

Whip up a batch of these crunchy, garlicky crisps to have on hand for spreads and dips or to crumble into soups.

3 tablespoons olive oil

3 cloves garlic, pushed through a press

2 cups Atkins Quick Quisine™ Bake Mix

1 tablespoon baking powder

½ teaspoon salt

1 cup club soda

2 eggs, lightly beaten

1 Heat oven to 350° F. Place olive oil and garlic in a small microwave-safe cup. Cook on high 1 minute or until garlic begins to turn golden; set aside.

2 Lightly coat an 8-inch by 4-inch loaf pan with vegetable oil. In a mixing bowl, combine bake mix, baking powder, and salt. Add club soda, eggs, and 1 tablespoon garlic oil. Mix thoroughly by hand or with an electric beater. Transfer dough to prepared pan; smooth top. Bake 1 hour.

3 Transfer bread to a wire rack to cool 20 minutes. Increase oven temperature to 400° F. With a serrated knife, cut loaf into 20 thin slices. Place slices on a baking sheet. Brush with half the remaining garlic oil. Bake 7 minutes. Remove baking sheet from oven; flip slices and brush with remaining oil. Bake an additional 7 minutes, until golden and crisp.

4 Cool toasts completely before storing in an airtight container for up to 3 days. Toasts may be frozen, wrapped, for up to 2 months.

Garlic-Herb Crisps: Add ½ teaspoon dried oregano and ½ teaspoon dried basil to the dry ingredients.

Rosemary-Olive Crisps: Add 6 pitted, chopped oil-cured black olives and 1 teaspoon crumbled dried rosemary leaves to the dry ingredients.

CHEESE STRAWS

PER SERVING (3 STRAWS)
Net Carbs: 1 gram
Total Carbs: 2 grams
Fiber: 1 gram

Protein: 4 grams
Fat: 9 grams
Calories: 125

Servings: about 12
Prep time: 25 minutes
Chill time: 2 hours
Bake time: 12 minutes

This delightful recipe won a recent Atkins recipe contest. For a sweet version, omit the Parmesan, garlic powder, and garlic salt, and mix in a half-teaspoon of cinnamon and five packets of sugar substitute.

1 cup Atkins Quick Quisine™ Bake Mix

6 tablespoons unsalted butter, cut into pieces

½ teaspoon garlic powder

¾ cup shredded cheddar cheese

¼ cup grated Parmesan cheese

2 eggs, lightly beaten

Garlic salt, for sprinkling

1 Place bake mix, butter, and garlic powder in a food processor. Process until mixture resembles coarse crumbs.

2 Add cheeses and eggs. Pulse until dough comes together. Transfer dough onto a large piece of plastic wrap. Lightly knead to form a smooth dough.

3 Place second piece of wrap over dough. Press or roll dough to a 6-inch by 12-inch rectangle, about ½ inch thick. Refrigerate dough until very firm, at least 2 hours (or overnight). Dough may also be placed in freezer until very firm.

4 Heat oven to 375° F. Place dough horizontally on countertop. Remove top sheet of plastic from dough. Sprinkle with garlic salt; gently press into dough. With a sharp knife, cut dough into forty 6-inch-long strips.

5 Transfer strips to an ungreased baking sheet. Bake 12 to 15 minutes, until lightly browned. Slide "straws" onto a cooling rack. When cool, store in an airtight container.

TOMATO-CUCUMBER GUACAMOLE

PER SERVING

Net Carbs: 6.5 grams
Total Carbs: 11.5 grams
Fiber: 5 grams

Protein; 2.5 grams
Fat: 7 grams
Calories: 107

Servings: 8
Prep time: 15 minutes

This hearty salsa can be enjoyed as a side dish, a topping for salad greens, or a savory condiment for chicken, pork, or burgers. For freshest flavor and brightest color, serve immediately after preparing.

1 pint cherry or grape tomatoes, halved, or 2 medium tomatoes, coarsely chopped

2 medium cucumbers (or 1 large English cucumber), peeled and coarsely chopped

2 Haas avocados, coarsely chopped

¼ cup chopped red onion

1½ tablespoons lime juice

1 teaspoon grated lime rind

½ teaspoon ground cumin

Salt and pepper

In a bowl, toss tomatoes, cucumber, avocado, onion, lime juice, rind, and cumin. Add salt and pepper to taste.

BRUSCHETTA WITH TOMATOES AND BASIL

PER SERVING

Net Carbs: 5.5 grams
Total Carbs: 10.5 grams
Fiber: 5 grams

Protein: 7.5 grams
Fat: 12.5 grams
Calories: 175

Servings: 4
Prep time: 10 minutes
Cook time: 5 minutes

Our version of this popular Italian appetizer is made with low carb bread, of course. In such a simple recipe it's important to find the best ingredients: vine-ripened tomatoes and extra-virgin olive oil.

4 slices Atkins Bakery™ Ready-to-Eat Sliced White Bread

3 tablespoons extra-virgin olive oil

2 garlic cloves, pushed through a press

2 medium ripe tomatoes, seeded and diced

¼ cup fresh basil leaves, cut in slivers

Salt and pepper

1 Toast bread in the oven until golden. While bread is toasting, place olive oil and garlic in a small microwave-safe bowl. Cook on high 30 seconds or until garlic is fragrant.

2 Brush garlic oil on bread. Cut each slice in half. Evenly top toast halves with tomatoes and basil. Season to taste with salt and pepper.

SMOKED WHITEFISH–STUFFED CUCUMBERS

PER SERVING

Net Carbs: 2.5 grams
Total Carbs: 3 grams
Fiber: 0.5 gram

Protein: 11 grams
Fat: 5.5 grams
Calories: 98

Servings: 4
Prep time: 10 minutes

Perfect for Induction, this is finger-food at its best. It also makes a great lunch for two—just don't cut the cucumber halves in pieces and serve one half per person.

1 English cucumber, peeled and cut in half lengthwise

⅓ cup sour cream

2 tablespoons white horseradish, patted dry

½ teaspoon Tabasco® (optional)

6 ounces smoked whitefish, bones removed, flaked

2 tablespoons finely chopped parsley

1 Remove seeds from cucumber halves with a small spoon. In a bowl, mix sour cream, horseradish, and Tabasco until well combined. Stir in whitefish.

2 Fill cucumbers with whitefish mixture. Sprinkle with parsley. Cut each half into 1-inch pieces and transfer to a serving platter.

SMOKED TURKEY ROLL-UPS

PER SERVING

Net Carbs: 2.5 grams
Total Carbs: 2.5 grams
Fiber: 0 grams

Protein: 10.5 grams
Fat: 16 grams
Calories: 192

Servings: 4
Prep time: 10 minutes

Spicy watercress and sweet sun-dried tomatoes make for a memorable flavor combination.

⅓ cup mayonnaise

1 tablespoon chopped sun-dried tomatoes in oil

¼ teaspoon pepper

8 slices smoked turkey breast (about 8 ounces)

1 cup washed and dried watercress, large stems removed

1 Mix mayonnaise, sun-dried tomatoes, and pepper until well combined. Spread mixture evenly over turkey slices.

2 Top each slice with one-eighth of the watercress. Roll up tightly. Cut each roll into thirds on the diagonal.

Orange-Sour Cream Waffles, page 30

BREAKFAST & BRUNCH

The morning meal used to mean eggs, eggs, and more eggs. No more: In addition to omelets, frittatas, and soufflés, we offer pancakes, waffles, breakfast sandwiches, and muffins. Excellent low carb baking ingredients and ready-to-eat bread allow you to start the day many delicious ways.

ORANGE–SOUR CREAM WAFFLES

PER SERVING

3 4

Net Carbs: 11.5 grams
Total Carbs: 15 grams
Fiber: 3.5 grams

Protein: 10.5 grams
Fat: 11 grams
Calories: 192

Servings: 4
Prep time: 10 minutes
Cook time: 10 to 15 minutes

We substituted sour cream for water in this recipe and added a little orange rind for a tasty variation on Atkins Quick Quisine™ Pancake & Waffle Mix. Make a double batch and freeze half for quick weekday breakfasts.

½ cup Atkins Quick Quisine™ Pancake & Waffle Mix

1 tablespoon oil or melted butter

2 large eggs, lightly beaten

⅓ cup sour cream

3 teaspoons grated orange rind, divided

BLUEBERRY SAUCE:

2 cups fresh or frozen blueberries (12 ounces) without added sugar

1 tablespoon granular sugar substitute

1 Heat waffle iron. In a medium bowl, stir together waffle mix, oil, eggs, sour cream, and 2 teaspoons of the orange rind.

2 Pour approximately ¼ cup of batter in center of the waffle iron. Cook according to manufacturer's instructions until crisp and golden brown. Repeat until all the batter is used.

3 FOR SAUCE: Mix blueberries, sugar substitute, and remaining 1 teaspoon orange rind in medium pot over high heat. Stirring occasionally, bring to a boil. Reduce to low. Simmer 10 minutes, until berries have given off liquid and volume has been reduced to about 1½ cups.

4 Purée blueberry mixture with an immersion blender or regular blender. To serve, divide waffles on four plates and serve with blueberry sauce.

Atkins Tip: To keep prepared waffles warm and prevent them from getting soggy while you use up your batter, place them in a 200° F oven, directly on the oven racks.

BUTTERMILK-CINNAMON WAFFLES

PER SERVING

2
3 4

Net Carbs: 3.5 grams
Total Carbs: 5.5 grams
Fiber: 2 grams

Protein: 4 grams
Fat: 12 grams
Calories: 175

Servings: 8
Prep time: 10 minutes
Cook time: 10 to 15 minutes

The acid in buttermilk reacts with the baking soda to produce a taste similar to sourdough bread. Buttermilk is lower in carbs than regular milk.

1 cup Atkins Quick Quisine™ Bake Mix

3 packets sugar substitute

1 tablespoon baking powder

½ teaspoon baking soda

2 teaspoons cinnamon

¾ cup buttermilk

3 eggs, lightly beaten

6 tablespoons butter, melted

3 tablespoons Atkins™ Sugar Free Vanilla Syrup

Cold water as needed

1 Heat waffle iron. In a medium bowl, whisk together bake mix, sugar substitute, baking powder, baking soda, and cinnamon. Add buttermilk, eggs, butter, and syrup; mix well. Batter will be stiff. Add cold water 1 tablespoon at a time until batter is spoonable.

2 Place approximately 3 tablespoons of batter in center of the waffle iron. Cook according to manufacturer's instructions until crisp and dark golden brown. Repeat with remaining batter.

YELLOW SQUASH AND GRUYÈRE FRITTATA

PER SERVING

Net Carbs: 3 grams	Protein: 23 grams	Servings: 4
Total Carbs: 4.5 grams	Fat: 25.5 grams	Prep time: 10 minutes
Fiber: 1.5 grams	Calories: 344	Cook time: 10 minutes

The frittata gets a quick finish under the broiler. Ovenproof your skillet by wrapping the handle with a double layer of aluminum foil.

2 tablespoons butter, divided

2 medium yellow squash, cut into ¼-inch rounds (2½ cups)

1 packed tablespoon thinly sliced fresh sage or basil leaves

10 large eggs

¼ cup water

½ teaspoon salt

¾ cup coarsely shredded Gruyère cheese

1 Melt 1 tablespoon butter in 12-inch nonstick ovenproof skillet over medium-high heat. Add squash and sauté 8 minutes; stir in sage. Cook just 1 to 2 minutes more until tender and browned in spots.

2 Meanwhile, arrange oven rack 6 inches from heat source; heat broiler. Whisk eggs, water, and salt in a bowl. Melt remaining tablespoon butter in skillet; pour eggs over squash. Reduce heat to medium-low, cover, and cook until set on bottom and edges but the top is still loose, about 3 minutes. Sprinkle Gruyère evenly over the top.

3 Broil frittata until just set, about 1 minute. Cut into wedges to serve.

MINI CHOCOLATE CHIP MUFFINS

PER SERVING (1 MUFFIN)
Net Carbs: 2.5 grams
Total Carbs: 5 grams
Fiber: 1 gram

Protein: 3.5 grams
Fat: 4 grams
Calories: 65

Servings: 24
Prep time: 10 minutes
Bake time: 15 minutes

A quarter-cup of coarsely ground pecans, or another favorite nut, can be added to these muffins to make them even yummier.

1 cup Atkins Quick Quisine™ Bake Mix

¼ cup granular sugar substitute

¼ teaspoon salt

½ cup sour cream

2 tablespoons butter, melted and cooled

2 tablespoons heavy cream

2 tablespoons water

1 teaspoon vanilla extract

½ cup sugar-free chocolate chips

1 Heat oven to 350° F. Grease two 12-compartment mini muffin pans. In a bowl, whisk bake mix, sugar substitute, and salt to combine. In another bowl, whisk sour cream, butter, heavy cream, water, and vanilla to combine.

2 Add the sour cream mixture to the bake mix mixture. Stir until well combined. Fold in chips. Divide batter in pan compartments, using about 1 rounded tablespoon per muffin.

3 Bake 15 minutes, or until lightly browned on top and toothpick inserted in center comes out clean. Cool muffins in pans 10 minutes, then turn out onto wire racks to cool completely.

SMOKED SALMON–DILL SCRAMBLED EGGS

PER SERVING
Net Carbs: 2 grams
Total Carbs: 2 grams
Fiber: 0 grams

Protein: 21 grams
Fat: 28 grams
Calories: 347

Servings: 4
Prep time: 10 minutes
Cook time: 15 minutes

The addition of fresh dill and smoked salmon turns scrambled eggs into a filling meal. Serve with buttered, toasted low carb bread.

8 eggs

3 tablespoons heavy cream

1 tablespoon chopped fresh dill

½ teaspoon salt

4 tablespoons butter

4 green onions (all white and 2 inches green), thinly sliced

6 ounces thinly sliced smoked salmon, cut into strips

1 In a large bowl, beat eggs, cream, dill, and salt. Melt butter in a large skillet over medium heat. Add green onions; cook 8 minutes, until softened.

2 Pour in egg mixture; cook 3 to 4 minutes, stirring occasionally, until almost set. Mix in salmon, cook 1 minute more or until eggs reach desired doneness. Transfer to warmed plates.

CARROT-NUT MUFFINS

PER SERVING (1 MUFFIN)

Net Carbs: 6 grams
Total Carbs: 9 grams
Fiber: 3 grams

Protein: 5.5 grams
Fat: 27 grams
Calories: 312

Servings: 12
Prep time: 15 minutes
Bake time: 20 minutes

These tender muffins can be made ahead and frozen, though nothing beats a freshly baked batch. What a pleasing aroma to wake up to!

1 cup Atkins Quick Quisine™ Bake Mix

1 cup (scant) finely ground almonds

1½ cups granular sugar substitute

2 teaspoons cinnamon

1 teaspoon salt

1 teaspoon baking soda

½ teaspoon baking powder

1 cup vegetable oil

4 eggs

1 medium carrot, coarsely grated

2 teaspoons vanilla extract

1 Heat oven to 350° F. Grease two 6-cup muffin pans; set aside. In a large bowl, whisk together bake mix, ground almonds, sugar substitute, cinnamon, salt, baking soda, and baking powder.

2 In a medium bowl, mix vegetable oil, eggs, carrot, and vanilla extract. Pour carrot mixture into bake mix mixture. Mix well. Divide batter in muffin pans.

3 Bake 20 to 25 minutes until tops are golden brown and a cake tester inserted in centers comes out clean. Cool on wire rack.

SMOKED SALMON TEA SANDWICHES

PER SERVING
Net Carbs: 7 grams
Total Carbs: 15.5 grams
Fiber: 8.5 grams

Protein: 18 grams
Fat: 9.5 grams
Calories: 210

Servings: 2
Prep time: 5 minutes

Caper-infused cream cheese brings out the flavor of the fish. These tasty sandwiches can be made up to a day ahead.

1 ounce cream cheese

1 tablespoon capers, drained and lightly crushed

4 slices Atkins Bakery™ Ready-to-Eat Sliced Rye Bread, crusts removed

1 ounce smoked salmon

¼ small red onion, thinly sliced

Freshly ground pepper

1 Mix cream cheese with capers; spread on bread slices.

2 Top 2 bread slices each with half the salmon, half the red onion, and pepper to taste. Top each with a slice of bread. Cut each sandwich into quarters on the diagonal.

CHOCOLATE PANCAKES

PER SERVING
Net Carbs: 8.5 grams
Total Carbs: 9.5 grams
Fiber: 1 gram

Protein: 10 grams
Fat: 20.5 grams
Calories: 274

Servings: 2
Cook time: 20 minutes

For chocolate lovers, this is a delicious variation on a breakfast favorite. Try serving
with no-sugar-added raspberry preserves and a dollop of whipped cream.

½ cup Atkins Quick Quisine™ Bake Mix

1 tablespoon unsweetened cocoa powder

3 packets sugar substitute

½ teaspoon baking powder

¼ teaspoon salt

¾ cup milk

2 eggs, beaten

2 tablespoons melted butter

2 teaspoons chocolate extract

Vegetable oil for cooking

1 Whisk bake mix, cocoa powder, sugar substitute, baking powder, and salt. Add milk, eggs, butter, and extract; mix until smooth. Let batter rest 5 minutes.

2 Heat a large nonstick skillet over medium heat; lightly coat with vegetable oil. Use 2 tablespoons batter per pancake. Cook until small bubbles appear at edges; flip and cook 30 to 45 seconds more.

CANADIAN BLT SANDWICHES

PER SERVING
Net Carbs: 7.5 grams
Total Carbs: 16 grams
Fiber: 8.5 grams

Protein: 20 grams
Fat: 11.5 grams
Calories: 240

Servings: 2
Prep time: 5 minutes

Not your traditional BLT, this sophisticated mix of flavors and textures includes lean
Canadian bacon and tarragon mayonnaise.

4 slices Atkins Bakery™ Ready-to-Eat Sliced White Bread, crusts removed

1 tablespoon mayonnaise

1½ teaspoons chopped fresh tarragon

1 teaspoon prepared mustard

2 slices Canadian bacon, cooked

1 leaf Romaine lettuce, halved

½ small tomato, thinly sliced

Freshly ground pepper

1 With a rolling pin, flatten the bread. Mix mayonnaise, tarragon, and mustard; spread on bread slices.

2 Top 2 bread slices each with half the Canadian bacon, half the lettuce, and half the tomato slices. Season with pepper to taste. Top each with a slice of bread. Cut each sandwich in quarters on the diagonal.

CANTALOUPE, BERRY, AND GREEN TEA SOUP

PER SERVING
Net Carbs: 7
Total Carbs: 8.5 grams
Fiber: 1.5 grams

Protein: 1 gram
Fat: 0 grams
Calories: 36

Servings: 4
Prep time: 10 minutes

Green tea brings a touch of herbal flavor to this refreshing and colorful vitamin-rich fruit purée.

1½ cups ripe cold cantaloupe, cut into 1-inch chunks

1 cup ripe strawberries, hulled

½ cup cold sugar-free green tea beverage

8 fresh blackberries or small strawberries, for garnish

4 tiny mint sprigs, for garnish

1 In a blender, purée cantaloupe and strawberries. With blender running, add tea through feed tube and process until smooth.

2 Evenly divide soup in shallow bowls. Add 2 blackberries or strawberries in center of each bowl and place mint sprig between the berries for garnish.

CHEESE SOUFFLÉ

PER SERVING
Net Carbs: 4 grams
Total Carbs: 4.5 grams
Fiber: 0.5 grams

Protein: 18.5 grams
Fat: 37.5 grams
Calories: 428

Servings: 6
Prep time: 15 minutes
Bake/cook time: 40 minutes

While this soufflé works well with five eggs, it rises to impressive heights with six. Eggs are easier to separate into whites and yolks when they are cold; however, to achieve maximum volume in beaten whites, bring them to room temperature before beating.

¼ cup grated Parmesan cheese, divided

4 tablespoons butter

2 tablespoons soy flour

2 tablespoons whole-grain pastry flour

¾ cup heavy cream

¾ cup water

2 cups grated cheddar cheese

¼ teaspoon salt

⅛ teaspoon cayenne pepper

6 large eggs, separated

1 Heat oven to 350° F. Grease a 2-quart soufflé dish. Sprinkle dish with 2 tablespoons Parmesan cheese. Melt butter in a medium saucepan over medium heat. Stir in soy and pastry flours; mix well.

2 Slowly add cream and water to flour mixture, stirring constantly. Stir in remaining Parmesan, cheddar cheese, salt, and cayenne. Bring to a boil, stirring constantly. Remove from heat and whisk in egg yolks, one at a time.

3 With an electric mixer, beat egg whites until stiff. Fold whites into cheese mixture in three additions. Gently pour soufflé mixture into prepared dish. Bake 40 to 45 minutes, until a skewer inserted in middle comes out clean and soufflé is completely risen and browned. Serve immediately.

OLD-FASHIONED BREAD PUDDING

PER SERVING

Net Carbs: 8 grams
Total Carbs: 14.5 grams
Fiber: 6.5 grams

Protein: 16.5 grams
Fat: 21 grams
Calories: 289

Servings: 6
Prep time: 10 minutes
Bake/cook time: 1 hour
Chill time: 30 minutes

This classic dish has just the right balance of flavor and texture. Real vanilla bean adds excellent flavor and a sweet perfume, allowing the use of a bit less sugar substitute than might be expected. In a pinch, though, you may substitute one teaspoon of vanilla extract.

8 slices Atkins Bakery™ Ready-to-Eat Sliced White Bread

6 large eggs

½ cup granular sugar substitute

1 cup heavy cream

1 cup water

1 vanilla bean, split and scraped

1 (3-inch) cinnamon stick

1 Heat oven to 350° F. Generously butter a 9-inch square baking pan; set aside. Trim crusts from the bread (save crusts to make breadcrumbs) and cut into ½-inch cubes. Place cubes in a large bowl. In a medium bowl, whisk together eggs and sugar substitute; set aside.

2 In a medium saucepan over medium heat, stir together the cream, water, vanilla, and cinnamon stick. Cook, stirring, until the mixture just comes to a boil.

3 Whisk hot cream into egg mixture, then pour over the bread cubes. Let stand 10 minutes, turning occasionally with a rubber spatula.

4 Transfer pudding mixture to the prepared pan. Place pan in a larger roasting pan; fill the outer pan with enough hot water to come halfway up the sides of the pudding pan. Bake for about 1 hour, until set. Let cool for at least 30 minutes before cutting. Serve warm or chilled.

SCRAMBLED EGGS WITH SAUSAGE

PER SERVING
Net Carbs: 4.5
Total Carbs: 5
Fiber: 0.5 gram

Protein: 18.5 grams
Fat: 21.5 grams
Calories: 227

Servings: 2
Prep time: 10 minutes
Cook time: 10 minutes

Homey and delicious, this hearty breakfast will keep you satisfied until lunchtime.

4 eggs

½ teaspoon salt

¼ teaspoon cayenne pepper

1 tablespoon olive oil

½ green bell pepper, thinly sliced

½ small onion, thinly sliced

2 fully cooked breakfast sausages, thinly sliced

1 Beat eggs with salt and cayenne; set aside. Heat olive oil in a medium skillet over medium heat. Add bell pepper, onion, and sausage. Cook 5 to 7 minutes, until the vegetables are lightly browned.

2 Pour egg mixture into skillet. Cook, stirring with a wooden spoon, 2 to 3 minutes, until eggs are desired consistency.

MUSHROOM-FONTINA FRITTATA

PER SERVING
Net Carbs: 5 grams
Total Carbs: 6 grams
Fiber: 1 gram

Protein: 25 grams
Fat: 30 grams
Calories: 395

Servings: 4
Prep time: 10 minutes
Cook time: 15 minutes

Low-heat cooking keeps eggs tender and fluffy. For an interesting variation, if you are past Induction, substitute three-quarters of a cup of goat cheese for the fontina.

8 eggs

¼ cup water

1½ cups shredded fontina cheese

1 teaspoon minced fresh thyme

1 teaspoon minced fresh rosemary

2 tablespoons olive or canola oil, divided

½ pound button mushrooms, wiped clean

½ cup chopped onion

¼ teaspoon salt

1 Whisk eggs with water, 1 cup cheese, and the herbs in a large bowl; set aside.

2 Heat 1 tablespoon oil in a large ovenproof skillet over medium-high heat. Add mushrooms and onion; cover and cook 3 minutes. Uncover, cook 6 to 7 minutes more, until golden; sprinkle with salt and transfer to bowl.

3 Heat remaining oil in skillet over medium-high heat; add egg mixture and cook 1 minute. Reduce heat to medium-low, evenly add mushrooms over top, cover, and cook 5 to 6 minutes, until edges are puffed.

4 Meanwhile, heat broiler. Sprinkle top of frittata with remaining cheese (it will look slightly uncooked on top). Transfer skillet to broiler, and broil 4 to 5 inches from heat source 1 minute, until lightly browned.

SOUTHWEST SCRAMBLED EGG BURRITOS

PER SERVING
Net Carbs: 7 grams
Total Carbs: 16 grams
Fiber: 9 grams

Protein: 32 grams
Fat: 27.5 grams
Calories: 419

Servings: 4
Prep time: 10 minutes
Cook time: 10 minutes

With or without the wrap, this hearty breakfast dish is delicious. "New Mexico"–flavor sausage is a fully cooked turkey and chicken mix with fire-roasted red peppers and cilantro. If you cannot find it, you may substitute any fully cooked sausage of your choice.

8 large eggs

¼ cup water

3 links (about 3 ounces each) fully cooked "New Mexico"–flavor turkey and chicken sausage

1 tablespoon canola oil, divided

½ cup shredded Pepper Jack cheese

4 garlic-and-herb-flavored low carb tortillas, if desired

1 Whisk eggs and water in a large bowl.

2 With a sharp knife, score casing of sausage down one side and pull off. Coarsely chop filling.

3 Heat 1 teaspoon oil in 12-inch nonstick skillet over medium-high heat. Add sausage and cook just until lightly browned, 2 minutes; remove. Wipe out skillet.

4 Heat remaining 2 teaspoons oil in skillet over medium heat. Add egg mixture, then sausage over top, and cook just 1 minute, until starting to set on bottom. Start turning eggs over to scramble gently and allowing soft parts to set, cooking about 1 to 2 minutes. When eggs are almost cooked, sprinkle with cheese and finish cooking, just until set but not dry. Serve immediately or continue with step 5.

5 FOR TORTILLAS: Wipe out skillet and heat over medium-high heat. Toast tortillas in dry or lightly greased pan on one side until golden, 1 minute. Fill center of toasted side of each tortilla with ¾ cup egg mixture. Roll up and toast seam side down until lightly golden, 1 minute more.

CHICKEN AND EGG SALAD

PER SERVING
Net Carbs: 4.5 grams
Total Carbs: 5 grams
Fiber: 0.5 gram

Protein: 32 grams
Fat: 23 grams
Calories: 362

Servings: 4
Prep time: 10 minutes
Cook time: 10 minutes

We've combined two favorite brunch salads in this recipe, and added a touch of seafood seasoning for a little extra zip.

1 tablespoon olive oil

1¼ pounds boneless, skinless chicken breast, cut into ½-inch dice

¾ teaspoon salt, divided

5 tablespoons mayonnaise

2 tablespoons finely chopped red onion

1 tablespoon white wine vinegar

¼ teaspoon Old Bay® seasoning

2 large hard-boiled eggs

⅔ cup finely diced celery, including some leaves

1 Heat oil in 12-inch skillet over high heat; add chicken, sprinkle with ¼ teaspoon salt, and sauté, stirring as chicken browns, 5 to 7 minutes. Remove from heat; cool until warm.

2 Meanwhile, combine mayonnaise, onion, vinegar, remaining ½ teaspoon salt, and seasoning in large bowl.

3 Finely chop eggs; stir into mayonnaise mixture with celery. Fold in chicken. Serve immediately or refrigerate if desired.

STRAWBERRY-STUFFED FRENCH TOAST

PER SERVING

Net Carbs: 7.5 grams
Total Carbs: 17 grams
Fiber: 9.5 grams

Protein: 26.5 grams
Fat: 25 grams
Calories: 377

Servings: 8
Prep time: 20 minutes
Cook time: 15 minutes

For a special-occasion brunch or lazy Sunday morning, try this low carb version of a favorite breakfast treat.

1 loaf Atkins Kitchen™ Quick & Easy Country White Bread Mix (baked according to package directions)

8 ounces cream cheese, softened to room temperature

3 tablespoons Atkins™ Sugar Free Strawberry Syrup

½ cup chopped fresh strawberries

¼ teaspoon cinnamon

½ cup heavy cream mixed with ½ cup water

3 eggs

2 packets sugar substitute

1 teaspoon vanilla extract

¼ teaspoon salt

1 tablespoon butter or more if needed

1 tablespoon canola oil or more if needed

1 Heat oven to warm setting. Line a baking sheet with foil; place in oven. Cut loaf into 8 thick slices. Make a pocket in each slice, taking care not to cut through to opposite side.

2 In a bowl, mix cream cheese and syrup until blended; fold in berries and cinnamon. Evenly divide mixture into bread pockets.

3 Mix cream mixture, eggs, sugar substitute, vanilla, and salt in a shallow bowl. Dip bread slices two at a time into mixture until saturated.

4 Heat 1 tablespoon each butter and oil in a large nonstick skillet. Cook slices in batches, 5 to 6 minutes per side, until golden brown. Do not crowd skillet. Add more butter and oil to skillet as needed. Transfer cooked slices to baking sheet to keep warm while cooking remaining slices.

OMELETS WITH GOAT CHEESE AND TOMATO

PER SERVING

Net Carbs: 4 grams
Total Carbs: 4.5
Fiber: 0.5 grams

Protein: 4 grams
Fat: 17.5 grams
Calories: 289

Servings: 2
Prep time: 5 minutes
Cook time: 5 minutes

Fresh goat cheese is available in most supermarkets. Paired with fresh thyme and chopped tomato, it is a flavor combination popular in France.

4 eggs

1 tablespoon heavy cream

1 teaspoon chopped fresh thyme leaves, or ½ teaspoon dried

½ teaspoon salt

¼ teaspoon pepper

1 tablespoon butter

2 ounces fresh goat cheese, crumbled

1 small tomato, seeded and finely chopped

1 In a bowl, beat eggs, cream, thyme, salt, and pepper.

2 Melt butter in a medium skillet over medium heat. Pour in egg mixture. Let set 1 minute, push eggs to one side with a spatula, tilt pan, and let uncooked eggs slide onto skillet.

3 Sprinkle goat cheese and tomato along set side of eggs. Fold eggs over filling; cook 2 minutes more. Slide onto a serving plate; cut in two. Serve immediately.

BACON, AVOCADO, AND CHEESE OMELETS

PER SERVING

Net Carbs: 6 grams
Total Carbs: 8.5 grams
Fiber: 2.5 grams

Protein: 30 grams
Fat: 45 grams
Calories: 555

Servings: 2
Prep time: 10 minutes
Bake/cook time: 10 minutes

These omelets are great for brunch or a light lunch. You can double the salsa recipe and keep on hand to top burgers or broiled chicken breasts.

SALSA:

1 small tomato, chopped

3 green onions, finely chopped

½ jalapeño pepper, fresh or canned (seeded and finely chopped)

2 tablespoons chopped fresh cilantro

1 tablespoon fresh lime juice

Salt and pepper

OMELETS:

4 eggs

2 tablespoons heavy cream

Salt and pepper

1 tablespoon butter, divided

4 slices lean bacon, cooked until crisp, crumbled

½ small avocado, peeled, pitted, and sliced

½ cup grated Monterey Jack cheese

1 FOR SALSA: In small bowl, combine tomato, green onions, jalapeño, cilantro, and lime juice and mix well. Season to taste with salt and pepper.

2 FOR OMELETS: In medium bowl, whisk eggs with cream and season with salt and pepper. Melt half the butter in a small nonstick skillet over medium-high heat and, when foam subsides, add half the egg mixture. Tilt pan to coat bottom and cook 1 minute, until almost set. Sprinkle half the omelet with half the bacon, avocado, and cheese and cook 1 minute. Fold empty half of omelet over filling and slide omelet onto a plate. Keep warm.

3 Repeat with remaining butter, egg mixture, bacon, avocado, and cheese. Serve with salsa.

TOASTED PECAN–CANTALOUPE KEBOBS

PER SERVING

Net Carbs: 3.5 grams
Total Carbs: 4.5 grams
Fiber: 1 gram

Protein: 1 grams
Fat: 3.5 grams
Calories: 50

Servings: 8
Prep time: 15 minutes
Bake time: 9 minutes

Skewered melon with a crunchy nut coating is a sweet addition to any breakfast. If you prefer macadamia nuts, use them instead of pecans.

8 (12-inch) skewers

⅓ cup pecans

¼ teaspoon cinnamon

⅔ medium cantaloupe, seeded

1 Heat oven to 350° F. On a baking sheet, toast pecans 8 to 9 minutes, until golden; let cool. In a food processor, finely grind cooled pecans; pulse in cinnamon and transfer to a sheet of wax paper.

2 Cut cantaloupe into eight 1-inch–thick slices. Remove rind from 1 slice and cut melon into 4 chunks; thread the pieces onto a skewer. Repeat with remaining slices until you have 8 skewers. Press one side of the kebobs onto pecan mixture and transfer, pecan side up, onto a serving platter. Serve immediately.

Chicken Noodle Soup, page 44

SOUPS & STEWS

From sophisticated soups to comforting stews, this wide array of recipes from different culinary traditions boasts a contemporary twist: The high carb ingredients have been omitted but the fantastic flavors remain. Whether you warm up with a bowl of Chicken Noodle Soup or indulge in cool creamy Chilled Seafood Bisque, you'll find many palate-pleasing options.

CHICKEN NOODLE SOUP

PER SERVING
Net Carbs: 3.5 grams
Total Carbs: 8 grams
Fiber: 4.5 grams

Protein: 49 grams
Fat: 5.5 grams
Calories: 284

Servings: 4
Prep time: 15 minutes
Cook time: 40 minutes

This chicken noodle soup gets its bright flavor from a whisper of lemon rind and a squeeze of lemon juice. If you wish, substitute one can of reduced-sodium chicken broth for a cup and a half of the water.

2½- to 3-pound chicken, quartered

1 large onion, diced

2 carrots, cut into 1-inch pieces

2 ribs celery, cut into 1-inch pieces

4 cups water

4 ounces Atkins Quick Quisine™ Pasta Cuts, fettuccine shape, broken into 1-inch pieces

1 teaspoon grated lemon rind

1 teaspoon lemon juice

1¾ teaspoons salt

¼ teaspoon freshly ground pepper

1 Place chicken, onion, carrots, celery, and 4 cups of water in a large pot. Bring to a boil over high heat. Reduce heat to low and simmer 35 minutes, or until chicken is cooked through.

2 Meanwhile, bring a pot of salted water to a boil. Cook fettuccine according to package directions.

3 Pour soup through a strainer into a smaller pot. Reserve chicken and discard vegetables. When cool enough to handle, remove chicken from bones and cut into ⅓-inch cubes.

4 Add chicken cubes, fettuccine, lemon rind, juice, salt, and pepper to the pot. Stir well; cook 2 to 3 minutes over low heat to heat through.

SPRING FENNEL AND PEA SOUP

PER SERVING
Net Carbs: 6 grams
Total Carbs: 9 grams
Fiber: 3 grams

Protein: 3.5 grams
Fat: 5.5 grams
Calories: 93

Servings: 6
Prep time: 15 minutes
Cook time: 12 minutes
Chill time: 1 hour

Pale green fennel has the crunch of celery and a mild licorice flavor. When cooked, it adds body to soups and stews.

1 medium fennel bulb, with stalks and fronds

1 (14½-ounce) can chicken broth

3 cups water

1 (10-ounce) package frozen peas, thawed

⅓ cup heavy cream

1 teaspoon minced shallot

¾ teaspoon salt

1 tablespoon chopped fresh mint, for garnish

1 Coarsely chop fennel and place in a large saucepan. Add broth and water. Bring to a boil, reduce heat, and simmer 12 to 15 minutes, until aromatic. Strain broth into a large glass liquid-measuring cup and discard solids.

2 In a blender, starting on low and increasing to high, purée peas, cream, shallot, and salt until almost smooth. With blender on, add fennel broth gradually through feed tube and purée until smooth. Chill in an airtight container until just cool or cold. To serve, evenly divide in six shallow soup bowls; garnish with mint.

Atkins Tip: For a special presentation, choose a large fennel bulb and thinly slice enough to make 1 cup of matchsticks for garnish. (Use remainder for soup.) Mound one-quarter of the matchsticks in the center of each bowl and add a sprig of mint. Pour soup gently into bowls from the side.

FRENCH ONION SOUP

PER SERVING

Net Carbs: 8.5 grams
Total Carbs: 15 grams
Fiber: 6.5 grams

Protein: 29 grams
Fat: 29.5 grams
Calories: 449

Servings: 4
Prep time: 15 minutes
Cook time: 1 hour

The secret to onion soup is letting the onions brown s-l-o-w-l-y, to concentrate their sweetness. If you prefer your cheese over instead of under the soup (gratinéed), place a bread slice over the soup in flameproof bowls, top with cheese, and broil three to four minutes, until the cheese browns and bubbles.

3 tablespoons butter

2 onions, thinly sliced

2 tablespoons Atkins Quick Quisine™ Bake Mix

2 (14½-ounce) cans reduced-sodium chicken broth

½ cup white wine mixed with ½ to 1 cup water

4 slices Atkins Bakery™ Ready-to-Eat Sliced White Bread, crusts trimmed, toasted

½ pound Gruyère cheese, shredded

1 Melt butter in a large soup pot over medium-low heat. Add onions; cook 35 minutes, stirring occasionally, until onions are very soft and golden brown. Stir in bake mix.

2 Slowly whisk in one can of chicken broth; pour in remaining can. Add wine mixture. Bring to a boil over high heat; reduce heat to low and simmer, covered, 20 minutes.

3 Heat four soup bowls. Place one slice of toast at bottom of each bowl. Top with one-quarter of the cheese. Ladle soup into bowls.

LAMB AND VEGETABLE STEW

PER SERVING

Net Carbs: 6 grams
Total Carbs: 9.5 grams
Fiber: 3.5 grams

Protein: 40.5 grams
Fat: 15.5 grams
Calories: 363

Servings: 6
Prep time: 20 minutes
Cook time: 1 hour 30 minutes

Lamb stew meat (the shoulder cut) is tasty, inexpensive, and underused, at least on this side of the Atlantic. Try this recipe for a change of pace from the more usual beef.

½ cup Atkins Quick Quisine™ Bake Mix

1 teaspoon salt

½ teaspoon pepper

2 pounds lamb stew meat

2 tablespoons olive oil

2 garlic cloves, pushed through a press

1 teaspoon dried oregano leaves

1 (14½-ounce) can diced tomatoes

½ cup water

1 tablespoon red wine vinegar

1 packet sugar substitute

2 cups green beans, cut into 1-inch pieces

2 small yellow squash or zucchini, cut into 1-inch pieces

1 Mix bake mix, salt, and pepper in a plate. Dredge lamb pieces in mixture. In a large Dutch oven or pot with cover, heat oil over medium heat. Brown lamb in batches; transfer to a plate.

2 Add garlic and oregano to Dutch oven; cook 1 minute, stirring. Return lamb and accumulated juices to Dutch oven. Add tomatoes, water, vinegar, and sugar substitute. Bring to a boil; reduce heat to low and simmer 1 hour 15 minutes, until lamb is almost tender.

3 Add green beans and squash to Dutch oven; mix well. Cook, partially covered, 15 minutes, until vegetables are tender.

ASIAN CHICKEN AND MUSHROOM SOUP

PER SERVING

Net Carbs: 5.5 grams
Total Carbs: 10 grams
Fiber: 4.5 grams

Protein: 32.5 grams
Fat: 6.5 grams
Calories: 238

Servings: 6
Prep time: 25 minutes
Cook time: 10 minutes

If you use canned chicken broth and chicken from the deli, this soup can be ready in minutes. Fish sauce can be found in Asian markets, while sesame oil, chili oil, and rice vinegar are also available in most supermarkets.

4 (14½-ounce) cans reduced-sodium chicken broth or 8 cups chicken stock

12 ounces fresh shiitake mushrooms (about 20 large), stems removed, caps sliced, or mix of other exotic mushrooms

2 tablespoons minced peeled fresh ginger

4 tablespoons Asian fish sauce (nam pla)

2 tablespoons soy sauce

1 tablespoon sesame oil

½ teaspoon chili oil

1 (10-ounce) skinless chicken breast, boned, poached, and shredded

3 cups sliced bok choy (or baby spinach)

4 teaspoons rice vinegar

Salt

Freshly ground pepper

2 green onions, sliced (for garnish)

1 Bring broth, mushrooms, and ginger to a boil in a large pot. Reduce heat and simmer 3 minutes.

2 Add fish sauce, soy sauce, sesame oil, and chili oil; simmer 2 minutes. Add chicken and bok choy; simmer until bok choy is tender, about 2 minutes. Stir in rice vinegar. Season with salt and pepper.

3 Ladle soup into bowls. Sprinkle with green onions and serve.

BACON–CHEDDAR CHEESE SOUP

PER SERVING

Net Carbs: 7.5 grams
Total Carbs: 9 grams
Fiber: 1.5 grams

Protein: 29 grams
Fat: 44 grams
Calories: 567

Servings: 4
Prep time: 5 minutes
Cook time: 15 minutes

Sharp cheddar combined with the bite of dry mustard and the smoky taste of bacon makes a quick, tasty, and filling soup.

4 strips bacon

1 small onion, chopped

½ teaspoon dry mustard

¼ teaspoon freshly ground pepper

1 (14½-ounce) can reduced-sodium chicken broth

4 teaspoons ThickenThin™ Not Starch thickener

2 cups half-and-half

12 ounces shredded cheddar cheese

½ teaspoon paprika (optional)

1 In a large saucepan over medium heat, cook bacon 6 minutes, until crisp. Remove and drain on paper towels. Crumble bacon.

2 Add onion to bacon fat in saucepan; cook 3 minutes, until onion just begins to brown.

3 Add mustard, pepper, and broth. Bring to a boil. Reduce heat to low. Whisk in thickener. Add half-and-half, cheese, and paprika; stir until cheese is melted. Ladle soup into heated soup bowls. Garnish with crumbled bacon.

CREAMY GARLIC, ZUCCHINI, AND PEA SOUP

PER SERVING

Net Carbs: 7.5 grams
Total Carbs: 9 grams
Fiber: 1.5 grams

Protein: 5 grams
Fat: 7 grams
Calories: 114

Servings: 4
Prep time: 10 minutes
Cook time: 25 minutes

This delicate soup is equally good served hot or cold. Pernod, a French anise-flavored liqueur, imparts a delicious undertone, but the herbal flavor of fresh dill works just as well.

3 cups reduced-sodium chicken broth

⅓ cup peeled garlic cloves (about 8 large cloves)

1 medium zucchini, diced

½ cup frozen peas

¼ cup heavy cream

1 teaspoon Pernod or snipped fresh dill

½ teaspoon salt

¼ teaspoon white pepper (optional)

1 In a medium saucepan, bring broth and garlic to a simmer; partially cover and cook 16 minutes, until garlic is very tender.

2 Add zucchini and cook 6 to 8 minutes, until it is tender but still bright green. Add peas and cook 1 minute more.

3 With a slotted spoon, transfer solids to a blender and purée until smooth, adding only enough broth to process. Add remaining broth and the cream and blend until smooth. Add Pernod or dill, salt, and pepper. If serving hot, return to pot to heat through; if serving cold, refrigerate until chilled.

GARLICKY COLLARD GREENS SOUP

PER SERVING

Net Carbs: 10 grams
Total Carbs: 14 grams
Fiber: 4 grams

Protein: 28 grams
Fat: 30.5 grams
Calories: 439

Servings: 4
Prep time: 10 minutes
Cook time: 20 minutes

This hearty main-course soup is based on the traditional Portuguese soup caldo verde, but our version contains no potatoes.

1 pound mildly spicy Italian sausage, sliced

1 small yellow onion, chopped

2 cloves garlic, pushed through a press

1 (14½-ounce) can reduced-sodium chicken broth, plus 1 can water

2 (10-ounce) packages frozen collard greens or kale, thawed

Hot pepper sauce (optional)

1 In a large saucepan over medium heat, cook sausage slices until browned. Add onion; cook until softened, about 5 minutes. Add garlic and cook 1 minute more.

2 Stir in chicken broth and water. Bring to a boil over high heat. Reduce heat to medium and stir in collards. Cook 10 minutes, stirring occasionally. Spoon into bowls; add hot pepper sauce to taste, if desired.

BUTTERNUT SQUASH SOUP

PER SERVING

Net Carbs: 9.5 grams
3 4
Total Carbs: 13.5 grams
Fiber: 4 grams

Protein: 2.5 grams
Fat: 12.5 grams
Calories: 168

Servings: 6
Prep time: 15 minutes
Bake/cook time: 65 minutes

An immersion blender makes quick work of cream soups, and involves much less cleaning than regular blenders.

1 small butternut squash (about 1¼ pounds), peeled, seeded, and cut into 1-inch pieces

2 tablespoons olive oil, divided

½ teaspoon salt, divided

¼ teaspoon pepper, divided

2 yellow squash (about 1¼ pounds), cut into 1-inch pieces

¼ cup finely chopped onion

1½ teaspoons pumpkin pie spice (see Tip)

1 tablespoon tomato paste

2 (14½-ounce) cans vegetable or chicken broth

½ cup heavy cream

Pumpkin seeds (optional)

Sour cream (optional)

1 Heat oven to 450° F. Toss butternut squash with 1 tablespoon olive oil, ¼ teaspoon salt, and ⅛ teaspoon pepper. Arrange in a single layer on a baking sheet. Roast 15 minutes, turning once.

2 Toss yellow squash and onion with remaining oil, salt, and pepper. Add to baking sheet with butternut squash. Continue roasting 20 minutes, until all vegetables are tender.

3 In a large saucepan over medium heat, cook pumpkin pie spice, stirring constantly, 1 minute or until fragrant. Stir in tomato paste and cook 1 minute more. Add roasted vegetables and broth. Bring to a boil, reduce heat to low, and simmer 20 minutes. Stir in cream. Remove from heat. Purée soup with an immersion blender.

4 Heat gently to warm through. Season to taste with additional salt and pepper. To serve, divide soup in bowls and garnish with toasted pumpkin seeds and sour cream, if desired.

Atkins Tip: To make your own spice mixture, combine 1 teaspoon cinnamon, ¼ teaspoon ginger, ⅛ teaspoon each of allspice and nutmeg, and a pinch of ground cloves.

ROASTED CAULIFLOWER–ALMOND SOUP

PER SERVING
Net Carbs: 6.5 grams
Total Carbs: 11 grams
Fiber: 4.5 grams

Protein: 10 grams
Fat: 37 grams
Calories: 406

Servings: 8
Prep time: 20 minutes
Cook time: 1 hour 25 minutes

Roasting cauliflower brings out its sweetness and imparts a nutty undertone, which the almonds heighten. This rich, ivory-colored soup makes an elegant start to any meal.

1 head cauliflower, florets cut into ¼-inch slices

6 tablespoons olive oil, divided

½ teaspoon salt

¼ teaspoon freshly ground pepper

1 (8-ounce) package slivered almonds, divided

1 medium onion, chopped

6 cups reduced-sodium chicken broth

1 cup heavy cream

1 Heat oven to 450° F. Toss cauliflower floret slices with 3 tablespoons olive oil, salt, and pepper. Arrange in single layer on 2 baking sheets. Roast 45 minutes, until browned. Turn once or twice during cooking time.

2 Remove cauliflower from oven. Reduce temperature to 350° F. Arrange 2 tablespoons of almonds on a baking sheet and bake 5 minutes, until lightly browned; set aside.

3 Heat remaining 3 tablespoons of olive oil in a large pot over medium heat. Add onion and cook 5 minutes, until translucent. Add remaining almonds and cook, stirring, until lightly browned, about 5 minutes.

4 Add chicken broth and roasted cauliflower. Bring to a boil, reduce heat to low, and simmer 20 minutes.

5 In a food processor fitted with a steel blade (or in a blender), purée soup in batches. Return puréed soup to pot. Stir in cream and 1 cup water. Cook on low a few minutes, just to heat through. To serve, divide soup in bowls and garnish with toasted almonds.

THAI GREEN CHICKEN CURRY WITH NOODLES

PER SERVING
Net Carbs: 10.5 grams
Total Carbs: 22.5 grams
Fiber: 12 grams

Protein: 93 grams
Fat: 34.5 grams
Calories: 769

Servings: 4
Prep time: 15 minutes
Cook time: 15 minutes

When you're in the mood for an easy, exotic entrée, try this dish. Green curry paste (available in most supermarkets) is a super shortcut for preparing Asian and Indian food.

2 tablespoons canola or peanut oil

2 pounds boneless, skinless chicken breast halves, cut into ¼-inch slices

2 teaspoons salt

2 tablespoons prepared green curry paste

1 (14-ounce) can unsweetened coconut milk

1 cup chicken broth

1 cup cut green beans, cooked

8 ounces Atkins Quick Quisine™ Pasta Cuts, fettuccine shape, cooked per package directions

¼ cup chopped fresh basil

2 tablespoons fresh lime juice

2 green onions, thinly sliced

1 Heat oil in a large nonstick skillet over medium heat until hot but not smoking.

2 Sprinkle chicken with salt. Add to skillet and cook 3 to 4 minutes, stirring occasionally (do not let chicken brown). Stir in curry paste and mix to evenly coat chicken. Add coconut milk and broth. Bring to a simmer; cook 2 to 3 minutes.

3 Add green beans, fettuccine, and basil and cook 2 to 3 minutes more, just until heated through. Stir in lime juice and pour onto a serving platter. Sprinkle with green onions and serve immediately.

Atkins Tip: Be sure to buy unsweetened coconut milk and to shake the can well before opening.

SCALLOP SOUP WITH CILANTRO CREAM

PER SERVING

Net Carbs: 5 grams
Total Carbs: 6 grams
Fiber: 1 gram

Protein: 7.5 grams
Fat: 30.5 grams
Calories: 326

Servings: 4
Prep time: 10 minutes
Cook time: 20 minutes

The flavor of this deliciously different fresh seafood soup is enhanced by a swirl of cilantro cream.

2 tablespoons butter, divided

½ pound medium-size sea scallops

¾ teaspoon salt, divided

1 small onion, chopped

1 small carrot, chopped

1 rib celery, chopped

1 tablespoon tomato paste

1 (8-ounce) bottle clam juice plus ½ cup water

⅛ teaspoon cayenne pepper (optional)

1 cup heavy cream, divided

½ cup chopped fresh cilantro

1 teaspoon grated lemon rind

1 Melt 1 tablespoon of the butter in a medium saucepan over medium-high heat. Add the scallops, and sprinkle with ½ teaspoon salt. Cook scallops 2 to 3 minutes, until lightly golden. Remove from saucepan.

2 Melt remaining tablespoon of butter. Add onion, carrot, and celery; cook until softened, about 3 minutes. Add tomato paste; cook 1 minute. Add clam juice, water, and cayenne, if using. Bring to a boil. Reduce to a simmer. Cook 3 minutes to heat through.

3 Add ½ cup heavy cream and half the scallops to the saucepan. Cook 2 minutes. Purée soup in batches in a blender. Return to saucepan.

4 Purée cilantro, lemon rind, and remaining ½ cup cream and ¼ teaspoon salt in blender until smooth and creamy.

5 Divide soup among bowls. Top each with one-quarter of the cilantro cream and one-quarter of the remaining scallops.

ASPARAGUS-TARRAGON "CREAM" SOUP

PER SERVING
Net Carbs: 8 grams
Total Carbs: 10 grams
Fiber: 2 grams

Protein: 5.5 grams
Fat: 5 grams
Calories: 100

Servings: 8
Prep time: 25 minutes
Cook time: 30 minutes

This soup is the perfect start to an elegant dinner in spring. Asparagus and fresh tarragon are at their seasonal peak, and yield a beautiful pale green hue. For a lovely presentation, garnish the soup with whole tarragon leaves.

1 tablespoon olive oil

1 small onion, chopped

3 (14½-ounce) cans reduced-sodium chicken broth

2 pounds asparagus, cut into 1-inch pieces

3 ribs celery, thinly sliced

¼ teaspoon salt

¼ teaspoon freshly ground pepper

1 tablespoon chopped fresh tarragon, divided

¾ cup nondairy creamer (see Tip) or cream

1 Heat oil in a large pot over medium-high heat. Add onion and cook 5 minutes, until softened but not browned.

2 Add broth, asparagus, celery, salt, pepper, and half the tarragon to the pot. Bring to a boil. Lower heat, cover, and simmer 20 minutes, until asparagus is very tender.

3 In a blender, purée soup in batches until smooth. Return to pot. Add nondairy creamer and remaining tarragon. Heat soup through over medium heat.

Atkins Tip: Look for a nondairy creamer (such as one made of soy) without hydrogenated oils.

COOL PEPPER AND ZUCCHINI SOUP

PER SERVING
Net Carbs: 3 grams
Total Carbs: 4 grams
Fiber: 1 gram

Protein: 2 grams
Fat: 5.5 grams
Calories: 69

Servings: 4
Prep time: 15 minutes
Cook time: 2 minutes

A touch of curry adds a spicy note to this beautiful yellow soup. For a different presentation, serve in clear glass dessert bowls.

1 tablespoon extra-virgin olive oil

1 tablespoon finely chopped shallot

½ teaspoon curry powder

1 medium yellow bell pepper

2 teaspoons minced fresh cilantro

1 medium zucchini, peeled and coarsely chopped

¾ cup chicken broth, divided

¾ teaspoon salt

2 tablespoons sour cream, at room temperature

1 Heat oil in a small skillet over medium heat; add shallot and cook 1½ minutes, until softened. Add curry and cook 30 seconds. Cool.

2 Finely dice enough pepper to equal 4 tablespoons, toss with cilantro in a bowl, and set aside for garnish.

3 Coarsely chop remaining pepper and place in a blender with zucchini, ¼ cup broth, and salt. Purée mixture on low, increasing gradually to high, until it is as smooth as possible, scraping sides of blender as necessary. Add remaining broth and the shallot mixture (scrape skillet with a rubber spatula); purée until smooth. Add sour cream and pulse to blend lightly.

4 Evenly divide soup in shallow bowls. Sprinkle centers with pepper-cilantro garnish.

WINTER POT ROAST AND VEGETABLE PURÉE

PER SERVING
Net Carbs: 4.5 grams
Total Carbs: 7 grams
Fiber: 2.5 grams

Protein: 78 grams
Fat: 26.5 grams
Calories: 596

Servings: 6
Prep time: 15 minutes
Bake/cook time: 2½ hours
(largely unattended)

This soul satisfying meal-in-one dish is perfect when the temperature drops. Just add a green salad, and dinner is done.

1 (4½-pound) boneless chuck beef roast

1½ teaspoons salt, divided

½ teaspoon ground pepper

2 tablespoons olive oil, divided

2 tablespoons butter

2 small onions (about 8 ounces total), thinly sliced

4 small carrots (about 8 ounces total), cut into 1-inch chunks

1 small head cauliflower, cut into florets (about 3 cups)

2 teaspoons herbes de Provence, divided

¼ cup beef broth or water

2 teaspoons ThickenThin™ Not Starch thickener (optional)

1 Heat oven to 350° F. Season roast with 1 teaspoon salt and pepper. In a large Dutch oven heat 1 tablespoon oil over medium-high heat until it shimmers. Brown beef about 15 minutes, turning to sear all sides. Remove roast from pan and keep warm.

2 Melt butter in remaining tablespoon oil. Add onions, carrots, cauliflower, and 1 teaspoon herbes de Provence. Cook about 8 minutes, until onions are browned. Add broth and return meat to pot. Cover and cook 2 hours, until meat is fork tender.

3 Remove roast to a cutting board; tent with foil. To make gravy, strain cooking liquid through a sieve and spoon off top layer of fat. Whisk in remaining 1 teaspoon herbes de Provence and thickener, if using. Add any accumulated juices from the roast. Mix well until gravy is smooth.

4 Transfer vegetables to a food processor (or mash with a potato masher) along with remaining ½ teaspoon of salt. Purée until smooth.

5 Slice meat and serve with puréed vegetables and gravy.

CHICKEN, SAGE, AND HAM SOUP

PER SERVING
Net Carbs: 3 grams
Total Carbs: 3 grams
Fiber: 0 grams

Protein: 31.5 grams
Fat: 16 grams
Calories: 286

Servings: 4
Prep time: 5 minutes
Bake/cook time: 10 minutes

The ingredients in this quick-cooking soup are based on the Italian dish saltimbocca, which combines chicken with prosciutto (Italian salt-cured ham).

1 tablespoon olive oil

2 tablespoons chopped shallot

2 (14½-ounce) cans reduced-sodium chicken broth, plus 1 cup water

1 pound boneless, skinless chicken breasts, cut into ½-inch cubes

4 ounces ham, chopped

½ teaspoon dried sage leaves

1 lemon

½ teaspoon salt

½ teaspoon pepper

1 Heat oil in a large saucepan over medium heat. Add shallot; cook 1 minute, until softened. Add broth, water, chicken, ham, and sage. Bring to a boil. Reduce heat to low. Cook 5 minutes, until chicken is almost cooked through.

2 Add 1 teaspoon grated lemon rind, 2 teaspoons lemon juice, salt, and pepper. Cook 2 to 3 minutes more.

MISO SOUP WITH TOFU

PER SERVING

Net Carbs: 6 grams
Total Carbs: 9 grams
Fiber: 3 grams

Protein: 20.5 grams
Fat: 11 grams
Calories: 196

Servings: 4
Prep time: 10 minutes
Cook time: 10 minutes

Many supermarkets carry miso paste in the refrigerated foods aisle. If yours does not, most Asian groceries stock it. Or, you can purchase it online. With miso paste on hand, a warming tasty bowl of soup can be ready in minutes.

1 (14½-ounce) can vegetable broth mixed with
   1 can water

3 tablespoons red miso paste

1 pound firm tofu, cut into ⅓-inch cubes

4 green onions, thinly sliced on the diagonal

½ cup thinly sliced mushrooms

1 Bring broth and water to a boil in a saucepan. Place miso in a bowl; whisk in a ladleful of broth.

2 Pour miso mixture back into pan. Heat over medium until soup just comes to a simmer. Add tofu, green onions, and mushrooms. Cook 1 minute more, to heat through. Serve immediately.

QUICK FRENCH COUNTRY STEW

PER SERVING

Net Carbs: 5 grams
Total Carbs: 6 grams
Fiber: 1 gram

Protein: 46.5 grams
Fat: 14 grams
Calories: 359

Servings: 4
Prep time: 15 minutes
Cook time: 25 minutes

To turn a classic stew into a tasty weeknight dinner, we used boneless chicken thighs instead of the more traditional whole cut-up chicken.

4 teaspoons extra-virgin or pure olive oil, divided

2 pounds boneless skinless chicken thighs,
  cut into 2-inch chunks

½ teaspoon salt, divided

1 yellow onion, cut into thin wedges

1 red onion, cut into thin wedges

2 medium garlic cloves, pushed through a press

2 teaspoons minced fresh thyme or ½ teaspoon dried

1 cup reduced-sodium chicken broth, divided

1 tablespoon whole-wheat flour

⅓ cup dry red wine

1 tablespoon Dijon mustard

1 tablespoon chopped fresh parsley

1 Heat 1 teaspoon oil in a large nonstick skillet over high heat. Add chicken, sprinkle with ¼ teaspoon salt, and cook 2 to 3 minutes per side, until browned. Transfer to a plate.

2 Add remaining 3 teaspoons oil to skillet; reduce heat to medium. Add onions, cook 8 minutes, until lightly browned; add garlic and thyme and cook 1 minute more. While onions are cooking, transfer 2 tablespoons of the broth to a cup and stir in flour.

3 Add wine to skillet; let bubble 1 minute. Return chicken to skillet, add plain broth, and cover. Reduce heat to medium-low, and cook 12 minutes.

4 Stir in flour mixture and remaining ¼ teaspoon salt, bring to a boil, and cook 1 minute, until slightly thickened. Stir in mustard and sprinkle with parsley.

ROPA VIEJA

PER SERVING
Net Carbs: 4.5 grams
Total Carbs: 6 grams
Fiber: 1.5 grams

Protein: 37 grams
Fat: 20 grams
Calories: 265

Servings: 4
Prep time: 10 minutes
Cook time: 2 hours 20 minutes

Cuban in origin, the name of this dish means "old clothes" or "rags" because the meat, in its flavorful sauce, cooks until it is finely shredded.

1½ pounds flank steak or skirt steak

1¼ teaspoons salt, divided

¾ teaspoon freshly ground pepper, divided

2 tablespoons olive oil, divided

1 small onion, quartered

1 teaspoon jarred jalepeño pepper, chopped

1 teaspoon pumpkin pie spice

1½ cups frozen bell pepper strips

2 cups chopped canned tomatoes

1 Season steak with ¼ teaspoon salt and ½ teaspoon pepper. Heat 1 tablespoon oil in a large heavy saucepan over medium-high heat. Add steak and cook 5 minutes, turning once to brown. Add onion and enough water to cover. Cover the saucepan and simmer about 2 hours and 15 minutes, adding water if necessary, until meat is so tender it falls apart.

2 Remove meat from saucepan. Strain cooking liquid; discard onion. Shred the meat with hands or two forks; set aside.

3 Heat remaining tablespoon oil over medium-high heat. Add jalapeño pepper and spice, and cook 30 seconds, stirring, until fragrant. Add pepper strips, tomatoes, 2 cups of reserved cooking liquid, meat, and remaining 1 teaspoon salt and ½ teaspoon pepper. Mix well; cook 5 to 10 minutes more to heat through.

CHILLED SEAFOOD BISQUE

PER SERVING
Net Carbs: 2.5 grams
Total Carbs: 2.5 grams
Fiber: 0 grams

Protein: 4 grams
Fat: 19.5 grams
Calories: 198

Servings: 4
Prep time: 15 minutes
Cook time: 15 minutes
Chill time: 1 hour

This cream-colored soup, garnished with plump, pink diced shrimp, is creamy, fragrant, and elegant. The soup itself is made with only six ingredients.

1 tablespoon butter

⅓ cup finely chopped onion

¾ cup heavy cream

½-inch sprig fresh thyme, plus more for garnish

1 (27-ounce) can clam juice or 3 (8-ounce) bottles

6 large cleaned, cooked shrimp, diced

1 Melt butter in a 2-quart saucepan over medium-low heat. Add onion, cover, and cook 3 to 4 minutes, until translucent. Meanwhile, bring cream and thyme to a boil in a separate small saucepan, reduce heat slightly, and cook about 5 to 7 minutes, until reduced to ½ cup. Remove thyme and let cream cool.

2 Add clam juice to saucepan with onion and bring to a boil; reduce heat slightly and cook 5 minutes. Cool; stir in reduced cream. In a blender in two batches, starting on low and increasing to high, purée broth mixture until smooth. Chill in an airtight container until just cool or cold. Ladle soup into bowls; garnish each with diced shrimp and a small sprig of thyme.

A Different Chopped Salad page 62

SALADS & SIDES

Fresh and cooked vegetables are an integral part of doing Atkins. In the Induction phase, salad fixings and green vegetables are vital for their nutritional benefits, including fiber. In the later phases, you can also enjoy most other vegetables, including acorn squash with melted butter or a savory salad made with corn, mango, and black beans.

A DIFFERENT CHOPPED SALAD

PER SERVING
Net Carbs: 8 grams
Total Carbs: 11 grams
Fiber: 3 grams

Protein: 4 grams
Fat: 6 grams
Calories: 108

Servings: 8
Prep time: 20 minutes
Cook time: 7 minutes

Just a small amount of wild rice adds a delightfully chewy texture to this easy-to-make chopped salad. It can be made up to three days before serving.

2 tablespoons olive or vegetable oil

1 tablespoon red wine vinegar

¾ teaspoon salt

½ cup very thinly sliced red onion

1½ pounds fresh green beans, trimmed

1 small head radicchio, coarsely chopped

¾ cup cooked wild rice (about ⅓ cup uncooked)

½ cup extra-creamy or regular blue cheese, crumbled

1 In a large bowl, combine oil, vinegar, and salt; stir in onion and let stand until beans are ready.

2 In lightly salted boiling water, cook green beans 7 to 8 minutes, until tender but still bright green. Drain in a colander under cold running water; shake to drain excess moisture. Stack in bundles and cut into ½-inch pieces.

3 Place green beans, radicchio, rice, and blue cheese in a large bowl; toss with dressing to coat.

PANCETTA-FLAVORED BRAISED CABBAGE

PER SERVING
Net Carbs: 6
Total Carbs: 8.5 grams
Fiber: 2.5 grams

Protein: 2.5 grams
Fat: 10 grams
Calories: 128

Servings: 4
Prep time: 20 minutes
Cook time: 25 minutes

Any combination of cabbage and salt-cured pork delivers superb taste. In this refined version, we chose pancetta, and added some fennel for a sweet background note.

⅓ cup finely chopped pancetta (1½ ounces)

1 tablespoon olive oil

½ cup finely chopped onion

½ cup finely chopped fennel bulb

4 cups thinly sliced green cabbage

¼ cup reduced-sodium chicken broth

¼ teaspoon salt

¼ teaspoon red pepper flakes

1 teaspoon white wine vinegar

1 In a large skillet over medium-high heat, cook pancetta 3 to 4 minutes until browned and crisp. Transfer to a plate.

2 Add oil, onion, and fennel to skillet and cook 3 minutes, until lightly browned. Add cabbage, broth, salt, and red pepper. Reduce heat to medium; cover and cook 18 to 20 minutes, until tender. Stir in vinegar and pancetta.

Atkins Tip: Pancetta is salt-cured Italian bacon. It is available in the deli counter at most supermarkets.

GREEN BEANS WITH SUN-DRIED TOMATOES

PER SERVING

Net Carbs: 8 grams
Total Carbs: 11 grams
Fiber: 3 grams

Protein: 5.5 grams
Fat: 9 grams
Calories: 154

Servings: 6
Prep time: 15 minutes
Cook time: 10 minutes

The concentrated flavors of sun-dried tomatoes and goat cheese, plus leeks and white wine, elevate simple green beans to an elegant side dish.

1 pound green beans, trimmed and cut into 1-inch pieces

2 tablespoons extra-virgin olive oil

2 leeks, white and 1 inch green, thinly sliced

2 garlic cloves, finely chopped

½ cup white wine

2 tablespoons sun-dried tomatoes in oil, drained and coarsely chopped

2 teaspoons chopped fresh thyme or ¾ teaspoon dried

Salt and pepper

4 ounces soft goat cheese, crumbled

1 Cook green beans in lightly salted boiling water in a large saucepan until crisp-tender, about 5 minutes. Drain and cool.

2 Heat oil in a large skillet over medium-high heat. Add leeks and cook 5 minutes, until softened; add garlic and cook 1 minute more. Add wine, tomatoes, and thyme. Increase heat to high and bring to a boil. Boil 2 minutes, until most of the wine evaporates.

3 Mix in green beans. Season to taste with salt and pepper. Transfer to a bowl; gently stir in goat cheese. Serve immediately.

ACORN SQUASH WITH SPICED APPLESAUCE

PER SERVING

Net Carbs: 11 grams	Protein: 0.5 grams	Servings: 6
Total Carbs: 12.5 grams	Fat: 3 grams	Prep time: 10 minutes
Fiber: 1.5 grams	Calories: 72	Bake/cook time: 20 minutes

To make the squash easier to cut, microwave it whole for a minute. Trim the curved undersides of the squash pieces with a knife so they will lie flat and cook evenly.

1 acorn squash (about 1½ pounds), seeded and cut into 6 wedges

2 teaspoons olive oil

¼ teaspoon salt

⅛ teaspoon freshly ground pepper

¾ cup unsweetened chunky applesauce

2 teaspoons butter

⅛ teaspoon ground cinnamon

1 tablespoon Atkins Quick Quisine™ Sugar Free Pancake Syrup, warmed

1 Heat oven to 375° F. Brush squash with oil and sprinkle with salt and pepper. Place on a jelly-roll pan lined with aluminum foil. Bake about 20 minutes, until squash is fork-tender.

2 In a small saucepan, heat the applesauce. Stir in butter and cinnamon; cook 1 minute more.

3 Serve squash with a dollop of applesauce and a drizzle of syrup.

ZUCCHINI PANCAKE

PER SERVING
Net Carbs: 4 grams
Total Carbs: 6.5 grams
Fiber: 2.5 grams

Protein: 18 grams
Fat: 22.5 grams
Calories: 288

Servings: 4
Prep time: 15 minutes
Cook time: 20 minutes

You may substitute yellow squash for the zucchini, if you prefer, and add a pinch
or two of basil, oregano, or marjoram.

1 pound zucchini, trimmed and coarsely grated

1 cup grated dill-havarti cheese (about 4 ounces)

⅓ cup Atkins Quick Quisine™ Bake Mix

⅓ cup chopped fresh parsley

3 eggs, beaten

½ teaspoon salt

¼ teaspoon pepper

2 tablespoons olive oil

1 Heat oven to 350° F. Place grated zucchini in a colander. Mix cheese, bake mix, parsley, eggs, salt, and pepper in a large bowl. Squeeze out excess liquid from zucchini and add zucchini to cheese mixture. Stir to combine well.

2 In a 10-inch skillet, heat olive oil over medium heat until it shimmers. Add pancake mixture and press down to spread, forming an even layer. Cook 4 minutes or until bottom is set.

3 Transfer skillet to oven; bake 12 to 15 minutes, until middle is just set. Remove from oven and let cool slightly. Cut into wedges. When serving, flip each wedge over so the crispy bottom crust faces up.

WARM LENTILS AND CELERY

PER SERVING
Net Carbs: 5.5 grams
Total Carbs: 9 grams
Fiber: 3.5 grams

Protein: 3.5 grams
Fat: 5.5 grams
Calories: 93

Servings: 4
Prep time: 15 minutes
Cook time: 25 minutes

This unusual side dish combines lentils, celery, and flat-leaf parsley with a delicious
lemon vinaigrette. Cooking time on lentils varies. Test for doneness at intervals,
cooking just until the lentils are tender but still hold their shape.

¼ cup brown lentils

5 medium ribs celery, strings removed and sliced
    ½ inch thick on the diagonal

3 tablespoons fresh lemon juice

1 large clove garlic

¾ teaspoon salt

½ teaspoon Dijon mustard

¼ cup extra-virgin olive oil

⅓ cup loosely packed fresh flat-leaf parsley, leaves only

Salt and freshly ground pepper

1 Fill a medium saucepan halfway with water and bring to a boil. Add lentils and cook 18 to 23 minutes, until tender. Drain.

2 Meanwhile, bring another medium saucepan filled two-thirds with water to a boil; add celery and blanch 20 seconds. Immediately drain in a strainer and run cold water over celery until lukewarm.

3 FOR DRESSING: Process lemon juice, garlic, salt, and mustard in a blender on low speed. Gradually drizzle oil through feed tube, increasing speed to high until blended and smooth.

4 Toss celery, lentils, and parsley with dressing. Add salt and pepper to taste.

BABY GREENS WITH GRAPEFRUIT AND RED ONION

PER SERVING

Net Carbs: 9 grams

3 4

Total Carbs: 12.5 grams
Fiber: 3.5 grams

Protein: 2 grams
Fat: 10.5 grams
Calories: 144

Servings: 4
Prep time: 15 minutes

Simple but superb, this delicate salad of contrasting textures and flavors goes with just about any entrée.

2 small grapefruits

3 tablespoons extra-virgin olive oil

1½ teaspoons chopped fresh tarragon
   or ½ teaspoon dried

¼ teaspoon dry mustard

Salt

Freshly ground pepper

10 ounces baby greens (mesclun)

½ small red onion, thinly sliced

1 Peel grapefruits with a small sharp knife. Place each fruit upright on a cutting board and cut away the white pith that surrounds each section. Reserve 1½ tablespoons grapefruit juice for dressing.

2 Mix oil and grapefruit juice in a mixing bowl; add tarragon and mustard. Whisk to combine. Add salt and pepper to taste and whisk again.

3 Add greens and toss gently with grapefruit sections, red onion, and salad dressing.

Atkins Tip: Jars of fresh "supremes," citrus fruit sections minus the surrounding white membrane, are often sold in the produce department. You'll need about 12 sections for this recipe.

ZUCCHINI AND CORN SALAD

PER SERVING

3 4

Net Carbs: 6.5 grams
Total Carbs: 8.5 grams
Fiber: 2 grams

Protein: 2 grams
Fat: 2.5 grams
Calories: 60

Servings: 6
Prep time: 15 minutes
Cook time: 10 minutes

This New Mexican–inspired recipe makes a great filling for low carb tortillas and omelets. Depending on your carb threshold, you may mix in Monterey Jack cheese, lime juice, sour cream, tomatoes, or cilantro to taste.

1 tablespoon canola oil

1 small onion, chopped

1 jalapeño pepper, chopped

2 pounds zucchini, thinly sliced into ½-inch rounds

½ cup corn kernels

¾ teaspoon salt

½ teaspoon chili powder

3 to 4 tablespoons water

1 In a large skillet over medium heat, heat oil until it shimmers. Add onion and pepper. Cook 1 to 2 minutes, stirring, until onion is softened.

2 Add zucchini, corn, salt, and chili powder; mix well. Cook 5 minutes or until zucchini is softened. Add 3 to 4 tablespoons water, cover, and cook 2 minutes more, until zucchini is soft and tender.

ASPARAGUS WITH MUSTARD VINAIGRETTE

PER SERVING

2
3 4

Net Carbs: 5 grams
Total Carbs: 8.5 grams
Fiber: 3.5 grams

Protein: 5 grams
Fat: 19 grams
Calories: 211

Servings: 4
Prep time: 10 minutes
Cook time: 10 minutes

A perfect springtime dish, the natural sweetness of asparagus contrasts beautifully with this tart vinaigrette.

1 pound fresh asparagus, trimmed

¼ small onion, very finely chopped

2 tablespoons white wine vinegar

1 teaspoon Dijon mustard

½ packet sugar substitute

½ teaspoon salt

¼ teaspoon pepper

¼ cup olive oil

4 cups baby greens (mesclun)

¼ cup toasted walnuts or almonds

1 Steam asparagus until crisp-tender. Drain, and pat dry with paper towels. Set aside.

2 Combine onion, vinegar, mustard, sugar substitute, salt, and pepper in a mixing bowl. Gradually whisk in oil.

3 Divide salad mix on plates; arrange asparagus on top and drizzle with vinaigrette. Sprinkle with nuts.

FRENCH BISTRO SALAD

PER SERVING
Net Carbs: 4.5 grams
Total Carbs: 5 grams
Fiber: 0.5 gram

Protein: 27 grams
Fat: 60 grams
Calories: 661

Servings: 4
Prep time: 20 minutes
Cook time: 5 minutes

A variation of a standard dish in French bistros, this combination of bacon, eggs, and a well-dressed salad is delicious and filling.

DRESSING:

2 tablespoons fresh lemon juice

1 teaspoon mustard

¾ teaspoon salt

¼ teaspoon freshly ground pepper

½ cup extra-virgin olive oil

SALAD:

4 large eggs

12 thick slices of bacon

6 cups frisée, curly endive, or chicory, cleaned and torn

1 cup shredded Gruyère cheese

1 FOR DRESSING: Combine lemon juice, mustard, salt, and pepper in a blender. With motor running, slowly add olive oil. Remove and set aside.

2 FOR SALAD: Poach eggs in an egg poacher, shallow sauté pan, or microwave. Cook about 4 minutes in an egg poacher or 2 minutes in microwave, until whites are set but yolks are still runny. Place in ice water until ready to use.

3 Stack bacon and slice into 1-inch by ½-inch pieces. Place in a small saucepan of cold water, bring to a boil and blanch for 30 seconds; remove and drain. In a small, cold sauté pan, cook bacon over medium heat until nicely browned and crisp. Drain and set aside.

4 To assemble salads, toss the frisée with the dressing and divide evenly on plates. Sprinkle with bacon slices and shredded cheese. To quickly reheat eggs, immerse in simmering water for 30 seconds. Place one egg on top of each salad.

SPICY COLLARDS AND OKRA

PER SERVING
Net Carbs: 5.5 grams
Total Carbs: 11.5 grams
Fiber: 6 grams

Protein: 5.5 grams
Fat: 6 grams
Calories: 111

Servings: 8
Prep time: 20 minutes
Cook time: 30 minutes

This dish combines two favorite southern vegetables. Loaded with fiber, minerals, and iron, it is as nutritious as it is tasty.

2 large bunches of collard greens (4 pounds total), rinsed; stems removed and discarded

3 tablespoons olive oil

4 large garlic cloves, finely chopped

½ teaspoon red pepper flakes

¼ pound okra, trimmed and sliced into rounds

1½ cups chicken broth

½ teaspoon salt

1 Bring a large stockpot filled two-thirds with water to a boil; add collards and cook 2 minutes. Drain.

2 Heat oil in 12-inch skillet over medium heat. Add garlic and red pepper; cook 1 minute, until garlic is golden. Add okra and cook 4 to 5 minutes more.

3 Add broth and collards to skillet and bring to a simmer. Cook 20 minutes, turning collards occasionally, until tender. Stir in salt.

CUCUMBER, MANGO, AND BLACK BEAN SALAD

PER SERVING

Net Carbs: 9.5 grams

Total Carbs: 12.5 grams
Fiber: 3 grams

Protein: 2.5 grams
Fat: 0 grams
Calories: 57

Servings: 4
Prep time: 10 minutes
Marinating time: 10 minutes

Mangoes and black beans are high in nutrient-dense carbs and fiber. We mixed in cucumber to reduce the overall carb count. This salad would make a great accompaniment to any grilled food.

1 seedless cucumber, washed and cut into ½-inch dice

½ medium mango, cut into ⅓-inch dice

½ cup canned black beans, drained and rinsed

2 tablespoons fresh lime juice

2 tablespoons orange juice

1 tablespoon finely chopped fresh cilantro

¾ teaspoon salt

1 jalapeño pepper, seeded and finely chopped

1 In a large bowl, toss cucumber, mango, and black beans.

2 FOR DRESSING: In a small bowl, mix lime and orange juices, cilantro, salt, and pepper. Pour over cucumber mixture and toss well. Let stand 10 minutes for flavors to blend.

GINGER, ALMOND, AND GARLIC BROCCOLI

PER SERVING

Net Carbs: 5.5 grams
Total Carbs: 7 grams
Fiber: 1.5 grams

Protein: 2.5 grams
Fat: 9 grams
Calories: 117

Servings: 4
Prep time: 10 minutes
Cook time: 10 minutes

The ginger-garlic duo livens up the flavor of broccoli, and a crunch of almonds adds the finishing touch.

1 tablespoon canola oil

1 tablespoon dark sesame oil

2 tablespoons finely sliced peeled fresh ginger

2 tablespoons slivered almonds

2 garlic cloves, thinly sliced

1 bunch broccoli, cut into 1-inch florets, stems peeled and cut into ¼-inch-thick slices

¼ cup reduced-sodium chicken broth

1 tablespoon soy sauce

1 tablespoon white wine vinegar

1 In a large heavy skillet, heat oils over medium-high heat. Cook ginger, almonds, and garlic in oil about 3 minutes, until golden. Transfer mixture to a paper towel to drain.

2 Add broccoli to skillet and cook until crisp-tender, about 5 minutes. Stir in chicken broth, soy sauce, and vinegar. Bring to a boil, and cook until liquid is almost evaporated. Toss the broccoli with ginger mixture before serving.

Note: Use a sharp knife for easier slicing. A dull one can be hard to control because you have to exert more pressure.

MANHATTAN-STYLE CREAMED SPINACH

PER SERVING

Net Carbs: 2 grams
Total Carbs: 5 grams
Fiber: 3 grams

Protein: 3.5 grams
Fat: 9.5 grams
Calories: 114

Servings: 6
Prep time: 15 minutes
Bake/cook time: 20 minutes

In New York, this is a much-requested standard steak-house side dish. One taste and you'll know why. Freshly ground pepper and grated nutmeg make a big difference in this recipe.

1 tablespoon butter

½ small onion, chopped

2 green onions, chopped

½ cup reduced-sodium chicken broth

½ cup heavy cream

½ teaspoon salt

½ teaspoon freshly ground pepper

⅛ teaspoon freshly grated nutmeg

2 (10-ounce) packages frozen leaf spinach, thawed and squeezed dry

1 In a medium skillet, melt butter over low heat. Cook onion and green onions 5 minutes, until softened. Stir in broth, cream, salt, pepper, and nutmeg. Bring to a boil. Reduce heat to medium and cook 15 minutes, until liquid is reduced to ⅔ cup and is thick enough to coat the back of a spoon.

2 Chop spinach; add to sauce and mix very well. Cook, stirring occasionally, 5 minutes, until very hot.

BROCCOLI PURÉE WITH GARLIC BUTTER

PER SERVING

Net Carbs: 7 grams
Total Carbs: 8.5 grams
Fiber: 1.5 grams

Protein: 3 grams
Fat: 25 grams
Calories: 261

Servings: 6
Prep time: 25 minutes
Cook time: 10 minutes

This sophisticated yet simple dish can be made two days ahead and reheated, making it perfect for Thanksgiving or any other multi-course holiday meal.

2 tablespoons olive oil

3 large shallots, sliced (1 cup)

1 bunch broccoli, cut into florets

3 tablespoons butter

2 small garlic cloves, minced

1 cup heavy cream, warmed

½ teaspoon salt

⅛ teaspoon freshly ground pepper

1 Heat olive oil in a large pot over medium heat. Add shallots; cook, stirring frequently, about 12 minutes, until golden and crisp. Reduce heat halfway through cooking time. Transfer shallots to paper towels to absorb excess oil. Set aside.

2 In the same pot, bring 4 cups of lightly salted water to a boil over high heat. Add broccoli and cook 7 minutes, until tender. Drain broccoli.

3 In the same large pot over high heat, add butter and garlic. Cook, stirring constantly, about 3 minutes, until butter is just browned and fragrant. Remove from heat.

4 Place broccoli and browned butter in food processor fitted with a steel blade. With the processor running, purée broccoli, slowly adding cream. Process until very smooth.

5 Transfer to a serving bowl; stir in salt and pepper. Sprinkle with shallots.

STUFFED ARTICHOKES

PER SERVING
Net Carbs: 11 grams
Total Carbs: 23 grams
Fiber: 12 grams

Protein: 19 grams
Fat: 22.5 grams
Calories: 345

Servings: 4
Prep time: 20 minutes
Bake time: 90 minutes

If you've never prepared fresh artichokes, now is the time to learn. Our step-by-step instructions make it simple…and the result is well worth the effort.

4 slices Atkins Bakery™ Ready-to-Eat Sliced White Bread

4 whole fresh artichokes

1 tablespoon fresh lemon juice, divided

⅓ cup olive oil

¼ cup grated Parmesan cheese

¼ cup chopped fresh parsley

3 garlic cloves, finely chopped

1 Heat oven to 300° F. Place bread directly on middle oven rack. Bake 15 minutes, until dried out. Remove from oven; increase heat to 375° F. Place bread in food processor and process until small crumbs form.

2 While bread is baking, prepare artichokes. With a sharp knife, cut off artichoke stems. Snap off the toughest leaves at the base (usually the bottom layer or two).

3 Lay artichokes on their sides and cut about ¾ inch off the top. With a pair of kitchen scissors, cut off the pointed ends of the leaves. Remove the middle leaves from the artichokes to expose the fuzzy chokes. With a spoon, scoop out the chokes, being careful to stop at the smooth heart. Drizzle half the lemon juice on the artichokes.

4 In a medium bowl, combine the remaining lemon juice, breadcrumbs, oil, cheese, parsley, and garlic. Place artichokes in a 9-inch-square baking dish. Pour ½ inch of water into the dish. Stuff the center of the artichokes with the bread mixture. Cover tightly with foil.

5 Bake for 1 hour. Uncover and bake 15 minutes more, until center leaves pull off easily and filling is lightly browned.

ITALIAN DELI PASTA SALAD

PER SERVING
Net Carbs: 3.5 grams
Total Carbs: 9.5 grams
Fiber: 6 grams

Protein: 24.5 grams
Fat: 12 grams
Calories: 238

Servings: 8
Prep time: 15 minutes
Bake time: 20 minutes

Flavorful and fiery cherry peppers are tamed by the mildness of pasta. This salad is best served the day it is made, at room temperature.

1 (8-ounce) jar pickled mushrooms in vinegar marinade, mushrooms halved

⅓ cup hot cherry pepper slices, finely chopped

5 tablespoons extra-virgin or pure olive oil

2 large garlic cloves, pushed through a press

1 teaspoon salt

¼ cup coarsely chopped fresh flat-leaf parsley

12 ounces Atkins Quick Quisine™ Pasta Cuts, fusilli shape

¼ cup grated Parmesan cheese

1 In a large bowl, combine pickled mushrooms, cherry peppers, oil, garlic, salt, and parsley.

2 Cook pasta according to package directions. Drain in a colander and rinse briefly under cool water to bring to a warm temperature. Add to bowl and toss to combine ingredients. Sprinkle with cheese.

Atkins Tip: Freshly grated Parmesan cheese is much more flavorful than packaged grated cheese. Keep a plastic-wrapped piece tucked away in your refrigerator.

ASPARAGUS, LIMA BEAN, AND SALAMI SALAD

PER SERVING
Net Carbs: 5 grams
Total Carbs: 7 grams
Fiber: 2 grams

Protein: 4.5 grams
Fat: 2 grams
Calories: 96

Servings: 8
Prep time: 15 minutes
Cook time: 5 minutes

This combo is definitely unusual—but wait until you try it. Serve this salad at room temperature for best flavor. Either purchase a solid chunk of Genoa salami from the deli counter or cut up a cured mini-Genoa.

2 bunches asparagus (30 spears), trimmed and steamed

2 tablespoons extra-virgin or pure olive oil

1 large clove garlic, pushed through a press

1 teaspoon minced fresh rosemary

Freshly grated rind of 1 lemon

¾ teaspoon salt

1 cup frozen baby lima beans, cooked

2 ounces Genoa salami, cut into matchstick pieces (about ⅔ cup)

1 In lightly salted boiling water, cook asparagus 5 to 6 minutes, until tender but still bright green. Drain in a colander under cold running water; shake to drain excess moisture. Stack in bundles and cut into 1-inch pieces.

2 In a large bowl, combine oil, garlic, rosemary, lemon rind, and salt. Add asparagus, lima beans, and salami; toss to coat.

NO-COOK ZUCCHINI WITH PESTO AND RED PEPPER

PER SERVING
Net Carbs: 2 grams
Total Carbs: 3.5 grams
Fiber: 1.5 grams

Protein: 3 grams
Fat: 9.5 grams
Calories: 105

Servings: 6
Prep time: 10 minutes
Standing time: 1 hour

Pesto isn't just for pasta. Here, it serves as a dressing and marinade for thinly sliced zucchini and red pepper.

¼ cup prepared pesto

2 tablespoons olive oil

1 teaspoon fresh lemon juice

2 medium zucchini, cut into thin rounds

1 roasted red pepper (jarred), patted dry and cut into thin strips

1 In a small bowl, combine pesto, oil, and lemon juice; mix well.

2 Arrange zucchini slices, overlapping slightly, in a shallow bowl. Top with red pepper strips. Brush pesto mixture over slices. Cover and let stand at least 1 hour for flavors to blend.

TOUCHDOWN SALAD

PER SERVING

Net Carbs: 4.5 grams	Protein: 3 grams	Servings: 10
Total Carbs: 9 grams	Fat: 11.5 grams	Prep time: 20 minutes
Fiber: 4.5 grams	Calories: 138	

A blender makes quick work of the super-creamy dressing—which can be made up to an hour ahead. Chipotles en adobo are smoked jalepeño peppers mixed with tomato and spices. Packaged in small cans, they can be found in the ethnic foods section of most supermarkets.

DRESSING:

1 medium red onion, divided

2 medium avocados (12 ounces total), pitted, peeled, and cut into pieces

⅓ cup mayonnaise

3 tablespoons fresh lime juice

1 teaspoon minced chipotle chile en adobo

1¼ teaspoons salt

¼ teaspoon ground cumin

SALAD:

1 large (1 pound) head Romaine lettuce (about 8 packed cups)

1 large (1½ pounds) head iceberg lettuce (about 9 packed cups)

12 radishes, trimmed and sliced

3 medium tomatoes, cut into wedges

1 medium cucumber, seeded and sliced

1 FOR DRESSING: Finely chop 2 tablespoons of the onion; combine with the remaining dressing ingredients in a blender. Process until smooth, stopping to scrape sides as necessary.

2 FOR SALAD: Thinly slice the remainder of the onion and place in a large bowl. Add the lettuces, radishes, tomatoes, and cucumber, and toss.

3 Add dressing to vegetables and toss gently to coat. Mix in dressing just before serving for maximum crispness.

Atkins Tip: The dressing is also a great spread on a low carb tortilla; top with cheese and roll up.

LEMON-BASIL GREEN BEANS

PER SERVING

Net Carbs: 3.5 grams	Protein: 1.5 grams	Servings: 4
Total Carbs: 6 grams	Fat: 2.5 grams	Prep time: 5 minutes
Fiber: 2.5 grams	Calories: 48	Cook time: 5 minutes

The beauty of seasonal cooking is combining a few fresh ingredients at their peak of flavor. This simple recipe is big on taste.

1 pound green beans, trimmed

1 tablespoon butter

1½ teaspoons grated lemon rind

¼ teaspoon salt

⅛ teaspoon pepper

¼ cup fresh basil, thinly sliced

1 Bring a large pot of lightly salted water to a boil. Cook green beans 5 to 6 minutes, until barely tender. Drain into a colander.

2 In the same pot over medium heat, melt the butter. Add green beans, lemon rind, salt, and pepper; stir to coat. Remove from heat. Toss with basil and serve immediately.

TRI-COLOR SALAD

PER SERVING
Net Carbs: 1.5 grams
Total Carbs: 2.5 grams
Fiber: 1 gram

Protein: 1 gram
Fat: 10.5 grams
Calories: 106

Servings: 4
Prep time: 10 minutes

This pretty salad is a go-with-everything side dish. To make it a main course, add sliced chicken, canned tuna, or another form of protein.

DRESSING:

3 tablespoons extra-virgin olive oil

1 tablespoon balsamic vinegar (or red wine vinegar mixed with ½ packet sugar substitute)

½ teaspoon fresh lemon juice

½ teaspoon salt

¼ teaspoon pepper

SALAD:

1 head endive, thinly sliced on the diagonal

½ small head radicchio, cut into bite-sized pieces

½ small head Bibb lettuce, cut into bite-sized pieces

1 In a salad bowl, whisk together olive oil, balsamic vinegar, lemon juice, salt, and pepper.

2 Add endive, radicchio, and lettuce. Toss to coat with dressing.

ZUCCHINI AND JICAMA SALAD

PER SERVING
Net Carbs: 4 grams
Total Carbs: 6 grams
Fiber: 2 grams

Protein: 1.5 grams
Fat: 0 grams
Calories: 26

Servings: 8
Prep time: 15 minutes

Jicama is a baseball-size root vegetable similar in texture to a radish, but with a slightly sweet flavor. Low in carbs, jicama adds crunch and volume to salads and salsas.

½ cup finely chopped red onion

¼ cup chopped fresh cilantro

¼ cup fresh lime juice

¾ teaspoon salt

1 packet sugar substitute

1 jalapeño pepper, seeded and minced

2 large zucchini (1½ pounds), halved lengthwise and cut into ¼-inch slices

1 small yellow bell pepper, finely diced

1 cup peeled and finely diced jicama

1 In a large bowl, combine red onion, cilantro, lime juice, salt, sugar substitute, and jalapeño. Mix well.

2 Add zucchini, bell pepper, and jicama and toss well until vegetables are evenly coated.

Atkins Tip: This salad can be made up to a day ahead and kept refrigerated in an airtight container.

NOODLE PUDDING

PER SERVING

Net Carbs: 10 grams
Total Carbs: 18 grams
Fiber: 8 grams

Protein: 34.5 grams
Fat: 34.5 grams
Calories: 513

Servings: 10
Prep time: 15 minutes
Cook/bake time: 30 minutes

This versatile dish can be served warm from the oven or at room temperature. It can also be served during any part of the meal—as an appetizer, side dish, or dessert (accompanied by a fruit purée).

1 pound Atkins Quick Quisine™ Pasta Cuts, fettuccine shape, broken into 2-inch pieces

8 ounces cream cheese, softened

1 cup granular sugar substitute

3 eggs

1 cup sour cream

1 cup pecans, coarsely chopped

½ cup unsalted butter, melted

1½ teaspoons ground cinnamon

1 teaspoon vanilla extract

½ teaspoon salt

1 Grease a 9-inch by 13-inch baking dish. Heat oven to 350° F. In a large pot of boiling water, cook fettuccine according to package directions. Drain and place in a large bowl.

2 While the pasta is cooking, beat cream cheese with an electric mixer until soft and creamy. Add sugar substitute; beat until incorporated. Add eggs, one at a time, beating until incorporated. With a rubber spatula, mix in sour cream, pecans, butter, cinnamon, vanilla, and salt until well combined.

3 Pour cream cheese mixture over drained, hot noodles. Mix well. Pour noodle mixture into prepared dish and smooth top. Bake 30 minutes, until just set and a knife inserted near the middle comes out clean.

Chicken Cacciatore, page 80

POULTRY

Broiled, roasted, or sautéed; breasts, wings, legs, or whole: Chicken and turkey are always popular dinner choices—the more ways to prepare them, the better. Here, you'll find something for every occasion, from zesty Caesar Burgers for speedy weeknight suppers to easy dinner party fare, like Cornish Hens with Peach-Lime Glaze.

CHICKEN CACCIATORE

PER SERVING

Net Carbs: 5 grams
Total Carbs: 6.5 grams
Fiber: 1.5 grams

Protein: 49.5 grams
Fat: 34.5 grams
Calories: 560

Servings: 4
Prep time: 25 minutes
Cook time: 1 hour

This delicious dish is even better made a day ahead. Serve with steamed spaghetti squash or low carb pasta.

2 tablespoons olive oil

1 (3- to 3½-pound) chicken, cut into 8 pieces

½ yellow onion, thinly sliced

2 garlic cloves, chopped

2 teaspoons dried oregano

½ cup dry white wine

½ teaspoon salt

¼ teaspoon pepper

1½ cups canned plum tomatoes, coarsely chopped

1 In a large skillet, heat oil over medium-high heat. Brown chicken in batches, about 5 minutes per side. Transfer to a plate. Add onion, garlic, and oregano to pan; cook 5 minutes, until onion is softened. Add wine and bring to a boil, stirring to loosen any browned bits. Add salt and pepper.

2 Return chicken and accumulated juices to skillet. Cook about 2 minutes, until almost all the wine has evaporated. Add tomatoes. Cover, reduce heat to low, and simmer 30 minutes, until chicken is cooked through.

3 Transfer chicken to a serving platter. Cook sauce 5 minutes to thicken; spoon over chicken.

GRILLED CAESAR BURGERS

PER SERVING

Net Carbs: 2.5 grams
Total Carbs: 5 grams
Fiber: 2.5 grams

Protein: 44 grams
Fat: 16 grams
Calories: 342

Servings: 6
Prep time: 10 minutes
Cook time: 12 minutes

Our chicken burgers are seasoned "Caesar-style" and served with crunchy Romaine leaves and garlic toasts in this new take on an old favorite.

2 pounds ground chicken

1½ cups grated Parmesan cheese

¼ cup capers, drained, rinsed, and lightly mashed

¼ teaspoon ground pepper

6 leaves Romaine lettuce, torn into bite-size pieces

2 tablespoons low carb Caesar salad dressing

3 slices Atkins Bakery™ Ready-to-Eat Sliced White Bread

1 tablespoon olive oil

1 large garlic clove, halved lengthwise

1 Prepare a medium grill or heat broiler. Combine ground chicken, cheese, capers, and pepper. Form mixture into six 4-inch patties.

2 Grill patties covered over medium heat 6 to 7 minutes per side, until just cooked through. Meanwhile, toss lettuce with dressing.

3 Brush both sides of the bread slices with oil. Grill bread on edge of grate (not directly over heat source) 2 minutes per side, until toasted. Rub cut side of garlic clove over one side of each slice of toasted bread, then cut bread in half on the diagonal.

4 Spread lettuce on a platter. Lay garlic toasts over lettuce, and place burgers over toasts.

CHICKEN CORDON BLEU

PER SERVING

Net Carbs: 3 grams
Total Carbs: 4.5 grams
Fiber: 1.5 grams

Protein: 50 grams
Fat: 34 grams
Calories: 541

Servings: 4
Prep time: 25 minutes
Bake/cook time: 35 minutes

Quite similar to Italian chicken saltimbocca, this prosciutto-Gruyère–flavored chicken breast is one of the easiest gourmet dishes to make.

4 (6- to 7-ounce) boneless, skinless chicken breast halves

4 ounces thinly sliced prosciutto

4 ounces Gruyère cheese, cut in ½-inch strips

1 egg

¼ cup milk

¼ cup Atkins Quick Quisine™ Bake Mix

¼ cup finely ground almonds

¼ cup grated Parmesan cheese

½ teaspoon salt

½ teaspoon pepper

2 tablespoons butter

2 tablespoons canola oil

Lemon wedges

1 Heat oven to 400° F. Butterfly chicken breasts: Place each breast half on a cutting board and make a horizontal slit through the thicker side, cutting almost to the opposite side. Open breast to form two flaps.

2 Place a quarter of the prosciutto and Gruyère on one side of each breast half, leaving a ½-inch border. Fold chicken over filling.

3 In a shallow bowl, mix egg with milk. On a plate, combine bake mix, almonds, Parmesan, salt, and pepper. Carefully dip each piece of chicken first in milk mixture, then in crumb mixture to coat.

4 Place butter and oil on a rimmed baking sheet; melt in oven. Place chicken on baking sheet. Turn to coat in butter mixture. Bake about 35 minutes, turning once halfway through cooking time, until browned on the outside and cooked through. Serve with lemon wedges.

CHICKEN FLORENTINE WITH BEANS

PER SERVING
Net Carbs: 6 grams
3 4
Total Carbs: 11 grams
Fiber: 5 grams

Protein: 44.5 grams
Fat: 12 grams
Calories: 334

Servings: 4
Prep time: 10 minutes
Cook time: 15 minutes

Genovese pesto is made from a smaller leaf variety of basil, and is especially delicious. If you can't find it, any basil pesto is fine.

4 (6- to 7-ounce) boneless, skinless chicken breast halves

4 teaspoons prepared Genovese or regular basil pesto

½ teaspoon salt

⅛ teaspoon freshly ground pepper

1 tablespoon olive oil

1 cup chicken broth

¾ cup small white beans, rinsed and drained

¼ cup freshly grated Parmigiano-Reggiano or other Parmesan cheese

1 (7-ounce) microwavable bag or 6 packed cups fresh spinach leaves, cooked and drained

1 Make a 2-inch slit lengthwise along the thick side of each chicken breast, cutting almost to the other side to form a pocket. Stuff each pocket evenly with a teaspoon of pesto. Press pocket to close. Sprinkle chicken with salt and pepper.

2 Heat oil in large nonstick skillet over medium-high heat. Brown breasts 2 minutes per side, until golden. Reduce heat to medium-low. Add broth and beans, partially cover, and simmer 5 to 7 minutes, until chicken is just cooked through.

3 Stir cheese into beans. Serve chicken, beans, and sauce over spinach.

CHICKEN ADOBO

PER SERVING
Net Carbs: 6 grams
Total Carbs: 6.5 grams
Fiber: 0.5 gram

Protein: 46 grams
Fat: 33 grams
Calories: 515

Servings: 4
Prep time: 10 minutes
Marinating time: 1 hour
Cook time: 35 minutes

The tangy vinegar marinade called adobo reflects the Spanish influence on the cuisine of the Philippines. Islanders enjoy adobo-seasoned pork, too.

1 cup white vinegar

2 garlic cloves, pushed through a press

1 bay leaf

1½ teaspoons whole peppercorns, lightly crushed

½ cup reduced-sodium soy sauce

6 whole chicken legs, cut into drumstick and thigh pieces

1 cup water

3 tablespoons canola oil

1 In a large glass baking dish, mix vinegar, garlic, bay leaf, peppercorns, and soy sauce; add chicken and toss to coat. Cover with plastic wrap and marinate in the refrigerator 1 hour.

2 Transfer chicken and its marinade to a large saucepan. Add water and heat to boiling over high heat. Cover, reduce heat to low, and simmer 20 minutes. With tongs, transfer chicken to a plate to cool. Boil cooking liquid about 10 minutes, until it is reduced to 1 cup. Let sauce cool and strain into a small saucepan. Skim off fat and reheat.

3 Pat chicken dry with paper towels. In a large skillet, heat oil over high heat until very hot. Brown chicken in batches, about 2 minutes per side. Transfer to a deep platter and pour hot sauce over chicken.

CHICKEN WITH TOMATOES AND CAPERS

PER SERVING
Net Carbs: 1 gram
Total Carbs: 2 grams
Fiber: 1 gram

Protein: 68 grams
Fat: 12 grams
Calories: 403

Servings: 6
Prep time: 10 minutes
Cook time: 25 to 40 minutes

Sweet tomatoes and pungent capers balance the mild flavor of chicken. Rinsing the capers after draining them eliminates excess salt.

2 tablespoons olive oil, divided

4 pounds boneless, skinless chicken breast halves or thighs

Salt

Freshly ground pepper

3 green onions, sliced

2 garlic cloves, finely chopped

2 small tomatoes, chopped

½ cup reduced-sodium chicken broth

2 tablespoons capers, drained and rinsed

1 Heat 1 tablespoon oil in a large deep skillet over medium-high heat. Season the chicken lightly with salt and pepper; cook until cooked through, 5 to 6 minutes per side (if using thighs, 12 to 14 minutes per side). Transfer to a plate; cover and keep warm.

2 Add remaining 1 tablespoon oil, green onions, and garlic to same skillet. Cook 5 minutes, until onion is tender. Add tomatoes, broth, and capers; simmer about 8 minutes, until slightly thickened. Season with salt and pepper. Return chicken to skillet and coat with sauce.

STIR-FRIED THAI CHICKEN WITH BASIL

PER SERVING

Net Carbs: 2.5 grams
Total Carbs: 3 grams
Fiber: 0.5 gram

Protein: 40.5 grams
Fat: 9 grams
Calories: 264

Servings: 4
Marinating time: 30 minutes
Cook time: 25 minutes

Do not skip the fish sauce in this recipe—it adds lots of flavor. Fish sauce and Thai basil are both available in Asian markets. Thai basil is more fragrant than Italian.

1¾ pounds boneless, skinless chicken breast halves, cut into 2-inch by 1-inch pieces

2 tablespoons Asian fish sauce (nam pla or nuoc mam)

1 tablespoons soy sauce

1 tablespoon water

1 packet sugar substitute

2 tablespoons canola oil

3 green onions, thinly sliced

3 garlic cloves, finely chopped

¼ teaspoon red pepper flakes

1 cup lightly packed small basil leaves, preferably Thai variety

1 Combine chicken, fish sauce, soy sauce, water, and sugar substitute in a bowl and let stand 30 minutes.

2 Heat a large skillet over medium-high heat and add oil. Heat until hot but not smoking. Add green onions and stir-fry 2 minutes, until softened. Add garlic and red pepper and stir-fry 30 seconds.

3 Remove chicken from marinade with a slotted spoon and add to onion mixture. Stir-fry about 3 minutes, until chicken is almost cooked through. Add the marinade and stir-fry mixture 30 seconds, until liquid boils. Remove from heat and stir in basil. Transfer to serving bowl.

Atkins Tip: If you can't find nam pla locally, go to www.ethnicgrocer.com.

SANTA FE TURKEY MEATBALLS

PER SERVING

Net Carbs: 4.5 grams
Total Carbs: 7.5 grams
Fiber: 3 grams

Protein: 31 grams
Fat: 23.5 grams
Calories: 364

Servings: 4
Prep time: 20 minutes
Cook time: 20 minutes

These lightly spiced turkey meatballs with melted cheese centers are a nice change of pace from traditional meatballs.

1 tablespoon canola oil, divided

1 small onion, finely chopped

2 slices Atkins Bakery™ Ready-to-Eat Sliced White Bread, torn into small pieces

½ cup water

1 pound ground turkey

1 garlic clove, pushed through a press

1 teaspoon ground cumin

1 teaspoon salt

¼ teaspoon pepper

¼ pound Pepper Jack cheese or plain Monterey Jack, cut into 12 equal-sized cubes

½ cup sugar-free green salsa

½ cup reduced-sodium chicken broth

1 In a large nonstick skillet, heat 1 teaspoon oil over medium heat. Cook onion in oil 5 minutes, until softened; cool slightly. In a large bowl, soak bread in water until soft. Mix in turkey, garlic, cumin, salt, pepper, and onion. Divide mixture into 12 portions.

2 Insert a cheese cube into the center of each portion and form into balls (make sure cheese is completely enclosed).

3 Heat remaining 2 teaspoons oil over medium heat. Cook meatballs 5 minutes, turning to brown on all sides. Mix salsa and chicken broth. Add to skillet; reduce heat to medium-low. Simmer, covered, 10 minutes or until meatballs are cooked through. Transfer to a plate; spoon sauce over meatballs.

CORNISH HENS WITH PEACH-LIME GLAZE

PER SERVING

Net Carbs: 4 grams
Total Carbs: 4 grams
Fiber: 0 grams

Protein: 64 grams
Fat: 52 grams
Calories: 335

Servings: 6
Prep time: 15 minutes
Marinating time: 1 hour
Cook time: 30 minutes

A brief marination tenderizes these little birds and imparts a sweet-tart flavor. Removing the backbone shortens grilling time and ensures more even cooking.

3 (2-pound) Cornish game hens, split in half

½ teaspoon salt

¼ teaspoon pepper

½ cup no-sugar-added peach or apricot jam

⅓ cup fresh lime juice

1 teaspoon grated lime rind

3 cloves garlic, pushed through a press

3 tablespoons soy sauce

½ packet sugar substitute

1 With a sharp butcher's knife, remove backbones from hens. Rinse and pat dry. Sprinkle with salt and pepper.

2 In a large bowl, mix jam, lime juice, lime rind, garlic, soy sauce, and sugar substitute. Add hens; toss to coat. Marinate 1 hour, turning occasionally.

3 Heat grill to medium. Remove hens from glaze; reserve glaze. Place hens skin side down on greased grill grate, not directly over heat. Cover and cook 25 minutes, until no longer pink inside and juices run clear.

4 Put reserved glaze in a small saucepan; bring to a boil. Boil for 1 full minute. Place hens directly over heat source, skin side down, for 5 minutes, and brush with glaze for a crispy skin.

CRISPY BUTTERMILK FRIED CHICKEN

PER SERVING

Net Carbs: 3 grams
Total Carbs: 6 grams
Fiber: 3 grams

Protein: 46.5 grams
Fat: 37 grams
Calories: 620

Servings: 4
Prep time: 20 minutes
Marinating time: 3 hours
Cook time: 40 minutes

Don't skip the marinating step. It makes the chicken very tender. If you like your fried chicken a little spicy, add a good pinch of cayenne pepper or Creole seasoning to the bake mix. This recipe doubles easily.

1½ cups buttermilk

1 tablespoon fresh lemon juice

1 (3-pound) fryer chicken, cut into 8 pieces

1 cup Atkins Quick Quisine™ Bake Mix

1 teaspoon salt

½ teaspoon freshly ground pepper

Vegetable oil for frying

1 In a large bowl, mix buttermilk and lemon juice. Add chicken; toss to coat. Cover and refrigerate at least 3 hours.

2 Drain chicken and pat dry with paper towels. Place bake mix, salt, and pepper in a plastic or paper bag. In two batches, add chicken and shake to coat. Place chicken on wire rack and let dry 15 minutes.

3 Heat oven to 350° F. Heat ½ inch of oil in a large skillet and, in two batches, fry chicken 4 to 5 minutes per side, until browned. Drain on paper towels and place on a baking sheet. Bake 30 to 35 minutes, until chicken is cooked through; turn pieces halfway through baking time.

GRILLED CHICKEN AND VEGETABLES WITH BASIL

PER SERVING

Net Carbs: 7 grams
Total Carbs: 9 grams
Fiber: 2 grams

Protein: 43.5 grams
Fat: 28.5 grams
Calories: 471

Servings: 4
Prep time: 15 minutes
Marinating time: 1 hour
Cook time: 15 minutes

A garlic-shallot marinade and fresh basil turn this simple grilled dish into something really special. Scrub, but don't peel, the vegetables for grilling.

¼ cup chopped shallots

3 tablespoons olive oil

3 garlic cloves, chopped

1 teaspoon salt

½ teaspoon pepper

4 (6- to 7-ounce) boneless, skinless chicken breast halves

1 red bell pepper, seeded and quartered

1 medium zucchini, quartered lengthwise

1 medium yellow squash, quartered lengthwise

1 medium leek, root trimmed (not removed), halved lengthwise

¼ cup fresh basil, coarsely chopped

1 Mix shallots, olive oil, garlic, salt, and pepper in a large resealable plastic bag. Add chicken, bell pepper, zucchini, squash, and leek. Gently shake bag to coat chicken and vegetables with marinade. Marinate in refrigerator, 1 to 3 hours, turning occasionally.

2 Prepare a medium-low heat grill. Place chicken and vegetables on the grill. Grill zucchini, squash, and leeks 7 to 9 minutes, or until just tender, turning occasionally to brown all surfaces. Grill pepper 9 to 11 minutes, or until tender, turning once. Grill chicken 12 to 14 minutes, or until just cooked through, turning once.

3 Transfer chicken and vegetables to a serving platter. Sprinkle with basil and serve immediately.

INDIAN TIKKA CHICKEN

PER SERVING

Net Carbs: 1 gram
Total Carbs: 1 gram
Fiber: 0 grams

Protein: 40 grams
Fat: 6 grams
Calories: 228

Servings: 4
Prep time: 10 minutes
Marinating time: 4 hours
Bake time: 30 minutes

Yogurt tenderizes the chicken in this dish. This simple recipe is delicious served with cucumber salad.

4 to 6 wooden or bamboo skewers

¾ cup whole-milk plain yogurt

1 tablespoon minced peeled fresh ginger

1 tablespoon chopped fresh cilantro, plus additional
  for garnish

2 teaspoons chili powder

1 teaspoon ground coriander

1 teaspoon dried mint

1½ pounds boneless, skinless chicken breasts,
  cut into 1-inch cubes

1 tablespoon olive oil

½ teaspoon salt

Lime wedges for garnish

1 In a shallow bowl, combine yogurt, ginger, cilantro, chili powder, coriander, and mint and mix well. Add chicken, cover, and marinate in the refrigerator, 4 hours or overnight.

2 About 1 hour before cooking, remove chicken from refrigerator and bring to room temperature. Soak 4 to 6 thin wooden or bamboo skewers in water.

3 Heat oven to 375° F. Thread chicken on skewers, place on a baking sheet, and drizzle with oil. Sprinkle with salt. Bake 30 minutes, turning once halfway through cooking time, until golden brown and cooked through. Sprinkle with chopped cilantro and garnish with lime.

MUSTARD-ONION–SAUCED CORNISH HENS

PER SERVING

Net Carbs: 6 grams
Total Carbs: 7.5 grams
Fiber: 1.5 grams

Protein: 81 grams
Fat: 79 grams
Calories: 1,104

Servings: 2
Prep time: 10 minutes
Cook time: 50 minutes

While each hen is a serving, if you have a more moderate appetite, feel free to divide each bird in half. Cooking time will vary, depending on the size of the birds. Allow an extra 10 to 20 minutes for larger hens.

2 (1- to 1½-pound) Cornish game hens

2 tablespoons extra-virgin or pure olive oil, divided

1 teaspoon kosher salt or ½ teaspoon regular salt

½ teaspoon freshly ground pepper

1 medium onion, finely chopped

1 medium garlic clove, minced

3 tablespoons white wine

1½ tablespoons whole-grain mustard

1 teaspoon minced fresh thyme

1 Heat oven to 425° F. Arrange hens breast side up on a broiler pan. Drizzle 1 tablespoon of the oil over the hens, spreading over entire surface. Sprinkle with salt and pepper. Bake 20 minutes.

2 Meanwhile, heat remaining tablespoon oil in a small skillet over medium heat. Cook onion 5 minutes, until translucent. Add garlic and cook 1 minute more. Add wine and boil 30 seconds; stir in mustard and thyme and remove from heat.

3 Reduce oven temperature to 350° F. Spoon sauce over breasts of hens (try to keep the chunky part of mixture on top of the birds). Bake 10 to 20 minutes more, until juices inside the thigh joint run clear when pierced with a knife.

GINGERY GRILLED CHICKEN AND PEACHES

PER SERVING
Net Carbs: 6 grams
3 4
Total Carbs: 8 grams
Fiber: 2 grams

Protein: 39.5 grams
Fat: 37.5 grams
Calories: 530

Servings: 4
Prep time: 20 minutes
Cook time: 15 minutes

Ginger and rosemary add flavor to mild-tasting chicken breasts. Instead of grilling, you may broil the chicken.

DRESSING:

⅓ cup olive oil

2 tablespoons sherry vinegar

2 teaspoons grated peeled fresh ginger

1 teaspoon crumbled dried rosemary

¼ teaspoon red pepper flakes

¼ packet sugar substitute

¼ teaspoon salt

CHICKEN:

4 (6- to 7-ounce) boneless, skinless chicken breast halves

Salt and pepper

2 medium ripe peaches, halved and pitted

10 ounces Romaine lettuce or mixed greens, cleaned

½ cup French feta or mild goat cheese, crumbled

1 Heat grill to medium. FOR DRESSING: Whisk together all ingredients. Set aside 1 tablespoon dressing to brush on chicken.

2 FOR CHICKEN: Sprinkle chicken with salt and pepper; brush with reserved dressing. Let chicken stand for 15 minutes.

3 Grill chicken 15 minutes, turning once halfway through cooking time, until just cooked through. Place peaches, cut-side down, on grill for 5 minutes, until softened. Cut chicken on the diagonal into ⅓-inch-thick slices. Cut each peach half into 4 slices.

4 Toss greens with remaining dressing and divide on plates. Top each salad with one-quarter of the chicken slices and one-quarter of the peach slices. Sprinkle with the cheese.

MEXICAN CHICKEN SALAD

PER SERVING

Net Carbs: 9 grams
Total Carbs: 18.5 grams
Fiber: 9.5 grams

Protein: 26 grams
Fat: 29 grams
Calories: 424

Servings: 4
Prep time: 25 minutes
Cook time: 15 minutes

If you like spicy food, sprinkle cayenne pepper on the strips before baking.

SALAD:

1 (12-ounce) boneless chicken breast

Salt and pepper

1 low carb tortilla

1½ teaspoons olive oil

½ red bell pepper, coarsely chopped

½ cup canned black beans, drained and rinsed

½ small red onion, finely chopped

8 cups (about 5 ounces) mixed greens

⅓ cup chopped fresh cilantro

1 Haas avocado

2 tablespoons fresh lime juice

1 small tomato, coarsely chopped

Lime wedges (optional)

DRESSING:

⅓ cup olive oil

2 tablespoons fresh lime juice

1 teaspoon grated lime rind

1 garlic clove, pushed through a press

½ teaspoon chili powder

¼ teaspoon ground cumin

¼ teaspoon salt

1 FOR SALAD: Heat grill to medium or preheat broiler. Brush grill with oil. Season chicken breast with salt and pepper. Grill 15 minutes, or until cooked through, turning once halfway through cooking time. (Chicken may be made up to 1 day ahead. Cool before wrapping and refrigerating.) Let chicken cool to room temperature, then thinly slice on the diagonal.

2 Heat oven to 400° F. Brush tortilla with olive oil and cut into thirds. Stack thirds and slice into ⅓-inch strips. Spread out on a baking sheet and bake 10 minutes, until golden. Set aside to cool.

3 In a large bowl, toss red pepper, beans, onion, greens, cilantro, and cooled tortilla strips until evenly mixed.

4 FOR DRESSING: In a large bowl, whisk olive oil, lime juice, grated lime rind, garlic, chili powder, cumin, and salt.

5 Toss greens mixture with dressing until evenly coated. Peel and pit avocado, cut into thin slices, and toss with lime juice. For each portion, place one-quarter of the greens mixture on each plate. Top with one-quarter of the chicken slices, one-quarter of the chopped tomato, and one-quarter of the avocado slices. If desired, serve with lime wedges.

ROAST CHICKEN WITH VEGETABLE STUFFING

PER SERVING
Net Carbs: 3 grams
Total Carbs: 5.5 grams
Fiber: 2.5 grams

Protein: 53 grams
Fat: 34.5 grams
Calories: 550

Servings: 6
Prep time: 20 minutes
Cook time: 1½ hours

This traditional Sunday family dinner will fill your home with a wonderful aroma. The stuffing is great baked inside a turkey breast, too.

2 tablespoons butter

1 small carrot, finely chopped

1 large rib celery, finely chopped

1 cup thinly sliced fresh mushrooms

1 small onion, finely chopped

2 slices Atkins Bakery™ Ready-to-Eat Sliced Bread, toasted and cut into ½-inch cubes

½ teaspoon dried thyme, crushed

½ teaspoon salt

¼ teaspoon freshly ground pepper

¼ cup heavy cream

1 tablespoon olive oil

1 (5-pound) roasting chicken, rinsed and patted dry

1 Heat oven to 350° F. Melt butter in a large skillet over medium heat. Cook carrot, celery, mushrooms, and onion until vegetables are tender but not browned, about 5 minutes. Mix in bread cubes, thyme, salt, pepper, and cream.

2 Spoon stuffing mixture into body and neck cavities of chicken and cover with skin. Tuck wing tips under chicken and tie legs together with kitchen string.

3 Rub chicken with olive oil and place breast side up on a rack in a shallow roasting pan. Cover loosely with foil and bake 1 hour. Remove foil and bake about 15 minutes longer, until browned and an instant-read meat thermometer registers 170° F in center of stuffing and thickest part of the thigh. Loosely cover chicken with foil and let stand 10 minutes before carving.

TURKEY RATATOUILLE

PER SERVING
Net Carbs: 6.5 grams
Total Carbs: 9.5 grams
Fiber: 3 grams

Protein: 61.5 grams
Fat: 15.5 grams
Calories: 429

Servings: 4
Prep time: 15 minutes
Cook time: 15 minutes

For busy weeknights, try this one-dish solution. It's a delicious way to make good use of a summer garden surplus.

4 tablespoons olive oil, divided

2 pounds turkey cutlets

Salt and pepper

1 Japanese or small Italian eggplant, cut into ¾-inch cubes

1 small zucchini, cut into ¾-inch cubes

1 small red bell pepper, cut into ¾-inch pieces

1 cup sliced mushrooms

2 garlic cloves, pushed through a press

½ cup tomato purée (such as Pomi's)

1 teaspoon dried basil

¼ packet sugar substitute

1 Heat 1 tablespoon oil in a large skillet over medium heat. Sprinkle cutlets with salt and pepper. Cook cutlets 3 minutes per side, just until lightly golden and cooked through. Transfer to a plate.

2 Heat remaining oil in skillet. Add eggplant, zucchini, and bell pepper. Cook 5 minutes, stirring occasionally. Add mushrooms, garlic, tomato purée, basil, and sugar substitute. Mix well; bring to a boil. Cover, reduce heat to low, and simmer 5 minutes. Season to taste with salt and pepper.

3 Return turkey and accumulated juices to skillet. Cook, uncovered 2 to 3 minutes, until turkey is heated through.

Atkins Tip: Japanese or small Italian eggplants don't need to be salted and rinsed before cooking.

TURKEY TACOS

PER SERVING

Net Carbs: 8 grams
Total Carbs: 17.5 grams
Fiber: 9.5 grams

Protein: 29.5 grams
Fat: 18.5 grams
Calories: 335

Servings: 4
Prep time: 10 minutes
Cook time: 10 minutes

This quick and easy entrée can be on the table in less than 20 minutes. Try it as no-hassle fare at your next casual dinner party.

2 tablespoons plus 1 teaspoon olive oil, divided

1 pound turkey cutlets

1 tablespoon taco seasoning

⅓ cup sour cream

¼ cup chopped red onion

2 tablespoons chopped fresh cilantro

4 low carb tortillas (any flavor)

½ bell pepper (any color), cut into thin strips

¼ cup sugar-free salsa

1 Heat 1 tablespoon of oil in a large skillet. Sprinkle turkey cutlets with taco seasoning; cook 2 minutes per side or just until cooked through. Transfer turkey to a cutting board and cut into strips.

2 Add sour cream, onion, and cilantro to skillet. Cook 1 minute, stirring, until heated through. Return turkey strips and juices to skillet.

3 To crisp each tortilla, place 1 teaspoon of oil in a medium skillet and heat until very hot. Fry tortillas 1 minute per side. Fill each with one-quarter of the filling. Top with one-quarter of the pepper strips and 1 tablespoon of salsa.

CHICKEN AND BRAISED ESCAROLE

PER SERVING

Net Carbs: 4.5 grams
Total Carbs: 11 grams
Fiber: 6.5 grams

Protein: 36.5 grams
Fat: 21.5 grams
Calories: 386

Servings: 4
Prep time: 20 minutes
Cook time: 35 minutes

Tapenade is a boldly flavored olive paste made from brined black olives, capers, and anchovies. Look for it in the canned and jarred vegetable section of the supermarket.

1 large head escarole, trimmed, rinsed well, and spun dry

1 (15-ounce) can reduced-sodium chicken broth

1 cup diced tomatoes in juice

¼ teaspoon coarsely ground pepper or crushed pepper

1 tablespoon jarred tapenade (black olive paste), optional

8 chicken thighs

¼ cup fresh sage leaves

3 large garlic cloves

¾ teaspoon salt

1 Bring escarole and broth to a boil in large covered stockpot. Boil until escarole is wilted, about 2 minutes. Add tomatoes and pepper. Cover, reduce heat slightly, and cook 6 to 8 minutes until escarole is very tender. Stir in olive paste, if using. (Can be made up to 3 days ahead up to this point. Cool completely and store chilled in airtight container.)

2 Heat oven to 425° F. Position a large broiler pan in upper third of oven. Bake chicken, skin side up, 30 minutes, until browned.

3 While chicken is baking, chop sage, garlic, and salt together on board. Baste tops of chicken with drippings and sprinkle with sage mixture. Bake chicken 5 minutes more. To serve, pour escarole into large shallow bowl and top with chicken.

Atkins Tip: If your cooking pot isn't large enough for all of the escarole, fold in the extra leaves after the first ones have been reduced.

SPICY CHICKEN LEGS

PER SERVING

Net Carbs: 0 grams
Total Carbs: 1 gram
Fiber: 1 gram

Protein: 46 grams
Fat: 37.5 grams
Calories: 535

Servings: 4
Prep time: 10 minutes
Marinating time: 30 minutes
Bake time: 40 minutes

Using a dry marinade enhances flavor and tenderizes the chicken. You probably have all these spices in your pantry. If not, all are well worth having on hand.

2 tablespoons canola oil

2 teaspoons paprika

1 teaspoon dried thyme

1 teaspoon chili powder

½ teaspoon dried cumin

½ teaspoon garlic powder

½ teaspoon salt

½ teaspoon pepper

¼ teaspoon ground nutmeg

6 chicken legs with thighs, rinsed and patted dry

1 In a small bowl, mix oil and the spices. Rub chicken legs with spice mixture; arrange on a baking sheet. Refrigerate 30 minutes.

2 Heat oven to 350° F. Bake chicken 40 to 45 minutes or until cooked through.

ROAST TURKEY WITH PAN GRAVY

PER SERVING
Net Carbs: 0 grams
Total Carbs: 0 grams
Fiber: 0 grams

Protein: 84 grams
Fat: 22.5 grams
Calories: 562

Servings: 10
Prep time: 15 minutes
Marinating time: 6 hours
Bake time: 2 hours 45 minutes

The process of soaking the turkey in a salt-water solution before cooking is called brining, which ensures an exceptionally tender bird and moist white meat. If you don't have the time, simply lightly salt the bird and skip the brining step.

1 (12- to 14-pound) turkey, trimmed of fat, giblets removed

1½ gallons water

1½ cups kosher salt

6 packets sugar substitute

1 carrot, roughly chopped

1 rib celery, roughly chopped

1 medium onion, roughly chopped

4 tablespoons unsalted butter, melted

1 tablespoon ThickenThin™ Not Starch thickener

1 (15-ounce) can reduced-sodium chicken broth plus ¼ cup water

½ teaspoon crumbled dried sage leaves

1 Submerge turkey, breast side down, in a tub of 1½ gallons water mixed with the kosher salt and sugar substitute. Refrigerate 6 hours. Discard brine and pat turkey dry.

2 Heat oven to 400° F. Place half of the vegetables in turkey cavity; scatter remaining vegetables on bottom of a roasting pan. Tie turkey legs together with cotton twine. Arrange bird breast side down on rack in pan. Pour 1 cup water into pan. Roast turkey 45 minutes.

3 Baste turkey with pan juices. Lower oven temperature to 375° F; roast for 1½ hours more, basting every 30 minutes (add an extra ½ cup water to pan if necessary).

4 Carefully turn turkey over with oven mitts, so it is breast side up. Brush breast with butter. Roast 30 minutes more. Turkey is done when an instant-read thermometer inserted into the inner thigh reads 175° F. Transfer turkey to a large carving board with a trench to catch juices. Remove all vegetables and discard. Cover loosely with foil. Let rest for 20 to 30 minutes before carving.

5 While turkey is resting, prepare gravy: Pour excess fat from roasting pan. Place pan on two oven burners on medium. Stir in thickener, until dissolved. Pour in chicken broth, water, and sage; bring to a boil, scraping up brown bits on bottom of pan with a wooden spoon. Cook 2 to 3 minutes until mixture thickens.

SPICY TOMATO-JALAPEÑO CHICKEN BREASTS

PER SERVING
Net Carbs: 4 grams
Total Carbs: 4 grams
Fiber: 0 grams

Protein: 40 grams
Fat: 8 grams
Calories: 262

Servings: 4
Prep time: 10 minutes
Cook time: 15 minutes

This piquant entrée can be on the table in less than half an hour. Be sure not to let the sauce boil: The low simmer keeps the chicken tender. For extra heat, garnish with fresh sliced jalapeños.

4 (6- to 7-ounce) boneless, skinless chicken breast halves

Salt and pepper

1 tablespoon olive oil

1 (14½-ounce) can petite-cut diced tomatoes with zesty jalapeños (such as Del Monte's)

1 tablespoon capers, rinsed and drained

1 tablespoon minced fresh oregano or 1 teaspoon dried

1 Sprinkle chicken on both sides with salt and pepper. Heat oil in a 12-inch skillet over medium-high heat. Arrange chicken in a single layer and cook without moving 3 minutes, until browned. Turn and cook 2 to 3 minutes more.

2 Add tomatoes, capers, and oregano to skillet. Reduce heat to medium-low; cover and simmer 9 minutes until chicken is just cooked through. Transfer chicken to plates and spoon sauce over top.

SAGE CHICKEN WITH BELL PEPPER CURLS

PER SERVING

Net Carbs: 3 grams
Total Carbs: 4 grams
Fiber: 1 gram

Protein: 49 grams
Fat: 27.5 grams
Calories: 427

Servings: 4
Prep time: 10 minutes
Cook time: 35 minutes

Fresh sage is less piquant than dried, and pairs beautifully with poultry. To save time, you can cook the chicken and peppers simultaneously in separate skillets.

4 boneless chicken breast halves, with skin
   (about 2 pounds)

¾ teaspoon salt, divided

½ teaspoon freshly ground pepper, divided

12 fresh whole sage leaves, plus 1 teaspoon chopped

1 tablespoon butter

2 tablespoons canola oil, divided

2 bell peppers of any color(s), cut into thin strips

1 cup water

1 Sprinkle chicken with ½ teaspoon salt and ¼ teaspoon pepper. Use fingers to loosen the skin of each chicken breast half, then spread 3 sage leaves under the skin.

2 Heat oven to 200° F. In a large ovenproof skillet over medium-high heat, melt butter in 1 tablespoon oil. Cook chicken 7 to 10 minutes per side, until browned and cooked through. Transfer to a serving platter, tent with foil, and place in warm oven.

3 Wipe out skillet with a paper towel. Heat remaining tablespoon oil over medium-high heat until it shimmers. Add bell peppers; sprinkle with remaining salt and pepper. Add 1 cup of water to skillet. Cook peppers, partially covered, 20 minutes, until softened and curled. Stir in chopped sage during last 5 minutes of cooking time. Serve peppers over chicken.

Shrimp and Asparagus Teriyaki, page 98

FISH & SHELLFISH

An excellent source of omega-3 fatty acids, fish and shellfish should be part of your meal plans at least three times a week. Seafood is often more costly than other protein sources and not everyone is used to cooking it, so we've selected recipes that not only bring out the delicate flavors, but are a snap to prepare, even for the novice cook.

SHRIMP AND ASPARAGUS TERIYAKI

PER SERVING
Net Carbs: 3.5 grams
Total Carbs: 5 grams
Fiber: 1.5 grams

Protein: 28 grams
Fat: 6 grams
Calories: 185

Servings: 4
Prep time: 15 minutes
Cook time: 8 minutes

Not for the fainthearted, this delicious Asian dish is authentically hot. For a milder version, mix one teaspoon of the chili oil with two teaspoons vegetable or sesame oil.

1 tablespoon hot chili oil, divided

1½ pounds extra-large (20 per pound count) shrimp, peeled and deveined

1 bunch asparagus, trimmed and cut on the diagonal into 1-inch pieces

4 cups sliced bok choy

¼ cup Atkins Quick Quisine™ Teriyaki Sauce

1 Heat 1 teaspoon of the oil in a large skillet or wok over high heat. Cook the shrimp about 3 minutes, until opaque. Transfer to a plate.

2 Heat remaining 2 teaspoons oil and add the vegetables to the skillet. Stir-fry about 3 minutes, until brightly colored and tender-crisp. Add the sauce; return the shrimp to the skillet and cook 1 minute, just until heated through.

BREADED SCROD WITH BASIL AND MUSTARD

PER SERVING
Net Carbs: 3.5 grams
Total Carbs: 6.5 grams
Fiber: 3 grams

Protein: 29 grams
Fat: 22.5 grams
Calories: 341

Servings: 4
Prep time: 15 minutes
Bake/cook time: 12 minutes

Crispy homemade breadcrumbs top tender fish in this foolproof entrée. Any mild-flavored fish works well with the garlic, oregano, and basil combo. Adjust roasting time based on the thickness of the fillets.

4 center-cut scrod fillets (about ½ pound each)

¼ cup fresh lemon juice

Salt and pepper

4 slices Atkins Bakery™ Ready-to-Eat Sliced White Bread

3 garlic cloves

1 teaspoon dried oregano

⅓ cup plus 2 teaspoons olive oil

1 cup fresh basil leaves

2 teaspoons Dijon mustard

1 Heat oven to 400° F. Put fillets on rimmed cookie sheet. Pour juice over fillets and season with salt and pepper.

2 In food processor, process bread, garlic, and oregano until fine crumbs form (you can also make crumbs with a box grater, in which case, don't tear the bread). With machine running, pour in 2 teaspoons olive oil; process to combine.

3 Evenly divide crumb mixture and pat over fillets. Roast 12 minutes, until just cooked through.

4 While fish is cooking, make the sauce: In a blender, purée basil leaves with remaining ⅓ cup olive oil and a dash of salt and pepper. Press sauce through a fine-meshed sieve. Whisk in mustard and spoon sauce around fish. For a decorative presentation, put basil sauce in a plastic bag. Snip off a small corner and squeeze a swirl of sauce on each plate.

FISHERMAN'S SOUP

PER SERVING
Net Carbs: 3.5 grams
Total Carbs: 4 grams
Fiber: 0.5 grams

Protein: 50.5 grams
Fat: 12 grams
Calories: 353

Servings: 6
Prep time: 25 minutes
Cook time: 40 minutes

You can use a variety of fish for this festive soup. If you prefer not to use lobster, squid is a good substitute—just add at the last minute and cook briefly.

3 tablespoons olive oil, plus more for serving, if desired

½ cup chopped celery

2 garlic cloves, finely chopped

½ pound plum tomatoes, peeled and chopped, or 1 cup canned tomatoes, drained

¼ cup chopped fresh parsley, plus more for serving, if desired

1 tablespoon chopped fresh rosemary, or 1 teaspoon dried

½ teaspoon red pepper flakes

¾ cup dry white wine

6 cups water

6 (4-ounce) frozen lobster tails, cut on underside with scissors

1 pound firm, white fish fillets (such as cod, halibut, or sea bass), cut into 2-inch pieces

8 ounces medium raw shrimp, deveined

Sea salt or table salt

1 Heat 3 tablespoons olive oil in large soup pot over medium-low heat. Add celery and cook 5 minutes. Add garlic and cook 1 minute more.

2 Stir in tomatoes, ¼ cup parsley, rosemary, and red pepper. Cook 2 minutes. Add wine; cook until liquid evaporates. Add water and bring to a boil. Reduce heat; simmer 20 minutes.

3 Add frozen lobster tails and cook 4 minutes; add fish and cook 3 more minutes until fish is opaque in center. Add shrimp and cook 3 more minutes. Season to taste with salt.

4 Ladle soup into bowls. Sprinkle with additional parsley and drizzle with olive oil, if desired. Have a bowl handy for discarded lobster and shrimp shells.

SEA SCALLOPS AND LEMON PASTA

PER SERVING
Net Carbs: 9 grams
Total Carbs: 20 grams
Fiber: 11 grams

Protein: 66 grams
Fat: 28 grams
Calories: 593

Servings: 4
Prep time: 10 minutes
Cook time: 8 minutes

Dry scallops well before sautéeing, for a lovely crisp edge. For extra flavor, deglaze the scallop pan by adding a quarter-cup dry wine and cooking for a minute, then add the liquid to the pasta dish and toss before serving.

1 ¼ pounds sea scallops (about 20)

½ teaspoon salt

¼ teaspoon freshly ground pepper

3 tablespoons olive oil, divided

12 ounces Atkins Quick Quisine™ Pasta Cuts, any shape

⅓ cup mayonnaise

2 tablespoons fresh lemon juice

1 ½ teaspoons grated lemon rind

⅓ cup chopped fresh chives

1 Sprinkle scallops with salt and pepper. In a large nonstick skillet, heat half the oil over medium-high heat. When the oil shimmers, add half the scallops. Cook 4 to 5 minutes, turning once halfway through cooking time, until just cooked through (scallops should be opaque but not rubbery). Transfer to a platter. Tent lightly with foil to keep warm. Repeat with remaining scallops and oil.

2 Meanwhile, prepare pasta according to package directions. Reserve ¼ cup pasta cooking water and drain the rest. Toss pasta with mayonnaise, lemon juice, lemon rind, and chives.

3 Gently toss scallops and their accumulated juices with pasta. Add reserved pasta water if necessary to loosen sauce. Serve warm or at room temperature.

SALMON AND BROCCOLI WITH PEANUT SAUCE

PER SERVING
Net Carbs: 5.5 grams
Total Carbs: 9.5 grams
Fiber: 4 grams

Protein: 37.5 grams
Fat: 29 grams
Calories: 445

Servings: 4
Prep time: 15 minutes
Bake time: 17 minutes

This recipe features baked salmon fillets over greens and broccoli mixed with a rich peanut sauce. When you lift the salmon from its baking foil, the skin remains; discard with the foil. A blender makes quick work of the sauce.

SAUCE:

3 tablespoons unsweetened peanut butter

3 tablespoons chicken broth

2 tablespoons mayonnaise

1 tablespoon lite soy sauce

1 tablespoon dry sherry or sake

1½ teaspoons Asian hot chili garlic sauce

½ teaspoon grated peeled fresh ginger

1 small garlic clove, pushed through a press

1 packet sugar substitute

SALMON:

4 (5- to 6-ounce) center-cut salmon fillets with skin

4 cups lightly packed baby greens (mesclun)

4 cups broccoli florets, cooked until crisp-tender

1 FOR PEANUT SAUCE: Purée ingredients in blender until smooth.

2 FOR SALMON: Heat oven to 300° F. Line a jelly-roll pan with aluminum foil. Place fish skin side down on pan. Bake 17 to 18 minutes, until fish flakes easily with a fork and center is still slightly rosy.

3 Toss greens and broccoli with ¼ cup peanut sauce. Divide on plates. Top each salad with a piece of fish. Drizzle on remaining sauce.

RED SNAPPER, VEGETABLE, AND PESTO PACKETS

PER SERVING
Net Carbs: 5.5 grams
Total Carbs: 9 grams
Fiber: 3.5 grams

Protein: 32 grams
Fat: 21.5 grams
Calories: 353

Servings: 4
Prep time: 10 minutes
Bake time: 25 minutes

This is the perfect dish for warm-weather dining. It's easy, light, and takes advantage of summer veggies. The foil packets can be made ahead and refrigerated up to one day before baking.

½ cup pesto (store-bought or homemade)

1 tablespoon fresh lemon juice

1 tablespoon extra-virgin olive oil

½ teaspoon salt

4 (6-ounce) red snapper fillets

12 asparagus spears, cut into 2-inch pieces

2 small yellow squash, thinly sliced on diagonal

4 green onions, thinly sliced on diagonal

1 small red bell pepper, cut into thin strips

2 tablespoons pine nuts

1 Heat oven to 425° F. Combine pesto, lemon juice, olive oil, and salt in a large bowl. Gently spread half the mixture on fish, and toss vegetables with remaining mixture to coat.

2 Cut four 12-inch squares of heavy-duty aluminum foil; fold each square in half, then open again. Distribute vegetables evenly over one side of each square, leaving a 1-inch border; lay one fillet on top of each. Sprinkle with pine nuts. Seal and crimp edges to make packets.

3 Transfer packets to a baking sheet, and bake 25 minutes. Open packets directly on dinner plates.

ASIAN LOBSTER SALAD

PER SERVING
Net Carbs: 8.5 grams
Total Carbs: 10.5 grams
Fiber: 2 grams

Protein: 38 grams
Fat: 12.5 grams
Calories: 309

Servings: 2
Prep time: 15 minutes

Asian seasonings bring out the delicate flavor of fresh seafood. The salad base of bok choy, also known as Chinese cabbage, has a celery-like crunchiness.

SALAD:

¾ pound cooked lobster meat

2 cups thinly sliced bok choy

½ thinly sliced red bell pepper

4 green onions, thinly sliced

1 tablespoon toasted sesame seeds

DRESSING:

2 tablespoons unseasoned rice wine vinegar

2 tablespoons soy sauce

1 tablespoon vegetable oil

1 teaspoon dark sesame oil

1 teaspoon grated peeled fresh ginger

½ packet sugar substitute

1 Cut lobster meat into 1-inch pieces. Mix with cabbage, pepper, green onions, and sesame seeds.

2 In a small bowl, whisk together vinegar, soy sauce, vegetable and sesame oils, ginger, and sugar substitute. Pour dressing over salad. Toss gently to coat.

Atkins Tip: To cook a live lobster, plunge it into a pot of rapidly boiling salted water. Cover and cook 8 minutes for the first pound, plus 3 to 4 minutes for each additional pound. Remove from the water with tongs and allow to sit for 5 minutes before cracking open the shell. For a speedier—and equally delicious— salad, substitute an equal amount of poached chicken breast for the lobster.

CHINESE FISH FILLETS

PER SERVING
Net Carbs: 4 grams
Total Carbs: 5.5 grams
Fiber: 1.5 grams

Protein: 37 grams
Fat: 22.5 grams
Calories: 379

Servings: 4
Prep time: 15 minutes
Cook time: 10 minutes

This dish works equally well with catfish fillets, sea bass, or carp. The ingredients for the sauce can be found in the Asian food section of most supermarkets.

SAUCE:

1½ cups reduced-sodium chicken broth

4 teaspoons ThickenThin™ Not Starch thickener

4 teaspoons dark sesame oil

3 cloves garlic, pushed through a press

4 teaspoons grated peeled fresh ginger

2 tablespoons unseasoned rice wine vinegar

2 tablespoons soy sauce

1 packet sugar substitute

FISH:

4 (8-ounce) catfish fillets

2 green onions, thinly sliced

1 Heat broiler. FOR SAUCE: Mix broth and thickener in a small bowl; stir until thickener dissolves. Heat oil in a medium saucepan over medium heat. Stir-fry garlic and ginger 30 seconds; add rice wine vinegar, soy sauce, sugar substitute, and broth mixture. Bring to a boil. Cook, stirring constantly, 1 minute. Remove from heat.

2 FOR FISH:Brush fillets with sauce. Broil 3 minutes per side. Transfer to plates; top with remaining sauce. Garnish with green onions.

SALMON BURGERS

PER SERVING

Net Carbs: 1.5 grams
Total Carbs: 1.5 grams
Fiber: 0 grams

Protein: 30 grams
Fat: 23 grams
Calories: 329

Servings: 6
Prep time: 15 minutes
Chill time: 2 hours
Cook time: 6 minutes

Top these burgers with slices of cool cucumber for a perfect balance of textures and temperatures. In a pinch, you may substitute three six-ounce cans of canned salmon for the fresh.

BURGERS:

2 salmon fillets, skinned and chopped
   (about 1½ pounds)

2 tablespoons chopped red onion

1 egg

2 teaspoons grated lemon rind

2 tablespoons fresh lemon juice

½ teaspoon pepper

1 tablespoon olive oil

SAUCE:

2 ounces cream cheese

¼ cup heavy cream

¼ cup chopped fresh dill

¼ teaspoon salt

¼ teaspoon pepper

1 FOR BURGERS: Combine salmon, red onion, egg, rind, juice, and pepper. Form into six 4-inch patties. Chill at least 2 hours.

2 FOR SAUCE: In a small saucepan or microwave-safe bowl, melt cream cheese with heavy cream. Cool a few minutes. Stir in dill, salt, and pepper; set aside.

3 Heat oil in a large nonstick skillet over medium heat. Cook patties 3 minutes per side or until cooked through. Serve topped with sauce.

CITRUS-CHILI SHRIMP

PER SERVING

Net Carbs: 4 grams
Total Carbs: 4 grams
Fiber: 0 grams

Protein: 35 grams
Fat: 20 grams
Calories: 343

Servings: 4
Prep time: 15 minutes
Marinating time: 10 minutes
Cook time: 5 minutes

This marinade does double duty: first as a flavoring agent and then as a sauce. We suggest serving the shrimp over steamed asparagus spears for a light yet filling low carb meal.

⅓ cup plus 1 tablespoon olive oil, divided

⅓ cup fresh orange juice, divided

2 tablespoons grated orange rind

1 tablespoon fresh lime juice

½ teaspoon salt

¼ teaspoon red pepper flakes

¼ teaspoon chili powder

¼ teaspoon ground cumin

1½ pounds jumbo (16 to 20 count) shrimp, peeled and deveined

1 tablespoon butter

1 In a medium bowl, mix ⅓ cup olive oil, 3 tablespoons orange juice, orange rind, lime juice, salt, red pepper, chili powder, and cumin. Add shrimp and marinate 10 minutes.

2 In a large skillet over high heat, melt butter with remaining tablespoon of olive oil. With a slotted spoon, remove shrimp from marinade; reserve marinade. Add shrimp to skillet. Cook about 4 minutes, until no longer pink and just cooked through. Transfer shrimp to a serving plate.

3 Add reserved marinade to skillet; add remaining orange juice. Bring to a full boil; boil 1 minute. Drizzle flavored oil over shrimp.

GARLIC SHRIMP WITH AVOCADO DIP

PER SERVING

Net Carbs: 1.5 grams
Total Carbs: 3.5 grams
Fiber: 2 grams

Protein: 6 grams
Fat: 9.5 grams
Calories: 122

Servings: 8
Prep time: 15 minutes
Cook time: 5 minutes

Creamy, spicy avocado dip is a perfect partner for garlicky grilled shrimp. This delicious appetizer can be served piping hot from the grill or at room temperature.

8 (12-inch) skewers

2 medium ripe Haas avocados, pitted and peeled

3 tablespoons jalapeño hot sauce

½ teaspoon salt

24 peeled and deveined jumbo shrimp

1 tablespoon olive oil

1 large garlic clove, pushed through a press

Pinch cayenne pepper

1 Cut up avocados and place them directly into a food processor. Purée with hot sauce and salt until smooth. Set aside.

2 Heat grill to medium-high heat.

3 In a bowl, rub shrimp with oil, garlic, and cayenne. Thread 3 shrimp onto each of 8 skewers, leaving small spaces between shrimp. (If using wooden skewers, soak in water for 1 hour before using so they won't burn.)

4 Grill shrimp covered, about 2½ minutes per side, until golden and just cooked through. Serve with avocado dip.

MAHI-MAHI WITH CREOLE SAUCE

PER SERVING

Net Carbs: 2.5 grams
Total Carbs: 3 grams
Fiber: 0.5 gram

Protein: 42.5 grams
Fat: 8 grams
Calories: 261

Servings: 4
Prep time: 20 minutes
Cook time: 20 minutes

Mahi-mahi, also called dolphin fish, is found from Florida to Hawaii. It has a firm yet delicate texture, and stands up well to flavorful sauces. This dish may be prepared up to one day ahead and gently reheated in a warm oven.

4 (6- to 8-ounce) mahi-mahi fillets or other firm white fish

1 tablespoon fresh lemon juice

Salt and pepper

1 tablespoon butter

½ small onion, thinly sliced

½ small red bell pepper, cut into thin strips

½ small green bell pepper, cut into thin strips

½ cup chopped canned tomatoes, with juice

1 tablespoon chopped fresh cilantro

Hot pepper sauce, to taste

1 tablespoon olive oil

1 Sprinkle fish with lemon juice, salt, and pepper; set aside. In a saucepan over medium-high heat, melt butter. Cook onions and bell peppers 2 minutes, until barely tender.

2 Add tomatoes with their juice; reduce heat to medium and simmer 8 minutes, until sauce thickens. Stir in cilantro. Add pepper sauce to taste.

3 Heat oil in large nonstick skillet over high heat. Sauté fish 3 minutes per side, until cooked through. Transfer to a serving platter. Spoon sauce over fish.

CARIBBEAN SNAPPER WITH GREEN SAUCE

PER SERVING

Net Carbs: 4.5 grams
Total Carbs: 6 grams
Fiber: 1.5 grams

Protein: 44.5 grams
Fat: 20 grams
Calories: 388

Servings: 4
Prep time: 15 minutes
Bake time: 15 minutes

A cooked vegetable coating keeps the snapper moist and adds a lot of flavor. A quick cilantro-based green sauce adds the finishing touch.

1 tablespoon extra-virgin olive oil

¾ cup red bell pepper, cut into a ¼-inch dice

¾ cup green bell pepper, cut into a ¼-inch dice

½ cup diced onion

4 (7- to 8-ounce) snapper fillets

½ teaspoon salt

SAUCE:

¼ cup extra-virgin olive oil

1 cup lightly packed fresh cilantro leaves

1 teaspoon grated peeled fresh ginger

½ teaspoon salt

1 lime, quartered, for garnish

1 Heat oven to 400° F; line a baking sheet with aluminum foil.

2 Heat oil in a large nonstick skillet over medium-high heat. Add peppers and onion; cook 5 minutes, just until tender and lightly golden.

3 Place fish on baking sheet; sprinkle with salt. Divide pepper mixture over fish. Bake 10 to 12 minutes, until fish flakes.

4 Meanwhile, process sauce ingredients in a food processor or blender to a chunky purée. Transfer fish with vegetables to plates, top with sauce, and serve with a lime wedge.

BAKED SALMON WITH BOK CHOY

PER SERVING

Net Carbs: 4 grams
Total Carbs: 5.5 grams
Fiber: 1.5 grams

Protein: 48 grams
Fat: 25 grams
Calories: 447

Servings: 4
Prep time: 10 minutes
Cook time: 10 minutes

Baking the salmon at a high temperature gives it a thick, crunchy crust. Bok choy is a mild, quick-cooking green. Be sure to purchase sugar-free salsa for the purée.

2 tablespoons olive oil

1 tablespoon butter

2 pounds salmon fillet, cut into 4 portions

½ teaspoon salt

¼ teaspoon pepper

1½ pounds bok choy, cut into 1½-inch pieces

½ teaspoon grated lemon rind

RED PEPPER PURÉE:

¼ cup roasted red peppers, patted dry

¼ cup mild, chunky sugar-free salsa

1 Heat oven to 475° F. Place olive oil and butter in an ovenproof skillet large enough to hold fish in a single layer. Place in oven 3 minutes, until butter is melted.

2 Season fish with salt and pepper. Place fish flesh side down in prepared skillet. Bake 10 minutes, turning carefully once halfway through cooking time, until just cooked through. Remove from skillet; tent with foil.

3 Add bok choy and lemon rind to skillet. Stir to coat with pan's oil. Place in oven 1 minute, until leaves are wilted and stems are warmed through.

4 To make purée, blend peppers and salsa in a blender 30 seconds. Divide greens on plates; top each with a piece of fish. Dollop purée over fish.

PECAN-CRUSTED SALMON WITH SPINACH

PER SERVING

2 3 4

Net Carbs: 3.5 grams
Total Carbs: 6.5 grams
Fiber: 3 grams

Protein: 37.5 grams
Fat: 57.5 grams
Calories: 716

Servings: 4
Prep time: 15 minutes
Bake/cook time: 15 minutes

Spinach makes a light and tasty sauce for salmon, and it's high in antioxidants, too.

SAUCE:

1 cup packed chopped fresh spinach

¼ cup dry white wine

1 small shallot, finely chopped

1 cup heavy cream

Salt and pepper

SALMON:

½ cup pecans (about 2 ounces)

½ cup Atkins Quick Quisine™ Bake Mix

½ teaspoon dried basil

½ teaspoon salt

¼ teaspoon pepper

2 tablespoons butter, at room temperature

4 (6- to 8-ounce) salmon fillets

1 Mix spinach, wine, and shallot in a small saucepan. Cook over medium heat 3 minutes, until spinach wilts. Stir in cream. Cook 15 minutes. Cool slightly; purée sauce in blender until fairly smooth. Return to saucepan to heat; add salt and pepper to taste.

2 Heat oven to 350° F. In a food processor, pulse pecans, bake mix, basil, salt, and pepper until nuts are finely ground. Transfer to a bowl and mix in butter.

3 Grease a large baking sheet. Place salmon on sheet. Spread fillets evenly with pecan mixture. Bake 15 minutes, or until cooked through. Serve with sauce.

KALE, PANCETTA, AND SHRIMP

PER SERVING

Net Carbs: 6.5 grams
Total Carbs: 8 grams
Fiber: 1.5 grams

Protein: 31 grams
Fat: 10.5 grams
Calories: 252

Servings: 4
Prep time: 20 minutes
Cook time: 20 minutes

Rich in antioxidants, kale is delicious paired with shrimp. Depending on the size of the leaves, the cooking time for kale can vary, so simmer until just tender before adding the shrimp.

4 packed cups coarsely chopped kale leaves

2 tablespoons extra-virgin or pure olive oil

⅓ cup finely chopped pancetta

3 garlic cloves, finely chopped

¼ to ½ teaspoon red pepper flakes

1½ cups chicken broth

1½ pounds (21 to 25 count) peeled and deveined shrimp

1 Fill a large saucepan or Dutch oven two-thirds full with water and bring to a boil. Add kale and cook 3 to 4 minutes, until almost tender. Drain kale in colander and wipe out pan.

2 Heat olive oil in pan over medium-low heat. Add pancetta, garlic, and red pepper. Cook 4 to 5 minutes, stirring frequently, until pancetta and garlic are light golden. Add kale and broth, cover, and bring to a boil. Reduce heat to low and cook at a high simmer, 7 to 10 minutes, just until kale is tender.

3 Stir in shrimp. Cover and cook about 4 minutes more, until shrimp are just cooked through and opaque in the center.

ITALIAN SEAFOOD SALAD

PER SERVING

Net Carbs: 11 grams
Total Carbs: 11 grams
Fiber: 0 grams

Protein: 52 grams
Fat: 15 grams
Calories: 406

Servings: 4
Prep time: 20 minutes
Cook time: 10 minutes
Chill time: 2 hours

Seafood cooked just-so, in a lively vinaigrette. If you're not fond of squid, you can substitute an equal amount of shrimp.

1½ pounds mussels, scrubbed, beards removed

¾ pound octopus or squid, cut in rings or pieces

¾ pound medium shrimp, shelled and deveined

½ pound cooked crabmeat

3 tablespoons olive oil

1 tablespoon white wine vinegar

1 garlic clove, pushed through a press

½ teaspoon salt

¼ teaspoon pepper

8 Boston lettuce leaves

2 tablespoons chopped fresh parsley

½ lemon, thinly sliced

1 Bring 1 cup of water to a boil in a large saucepan with a cover. Add mussels; cook 10 minutes. Remove mussels from their shells and transfer to a large bowl. Discard any unopened mussels.

2 Bring 1 quart of lightly salted water to a boil. Add octopus; cook 45 seconds, just until opaque. Remove with a slotted spoon and add to bowl with mussels. In the same water, cook shrimp 2 to 3 minutes, just until cooked through. Remove with a slotted spoon and add to bowl. Stir in crab.

3 Add olive oil, vinegar, garlic, salt, and pepper to seafood. Mix until thoroughly combined. Refrigerate 2 hours for flavors to meld.

4 To serve, divide lettuce leaves on plates. Mound seafood salad over lettuce; sprinkle with parsley and garnish with lemon slices.

MEDITERRANEAN SWORDFISH STEAKS

PER SERVING
Net Carbs: 0.5 grams
Total Carbs: 0.5 grams
Fiber: 0 grams

Protein: 23 grams
Fat: 14.5 grams
Calories: 232

Servings: 4
Prep time: 5 minutes
Marinating time: 30 minutes
Cook time: 10 minutes

Meaty swordfish stands up to bold herbs like oregano and rosemary. The thirty-minute marinade guarantees flavorful, moist fish.

¼ cup olive oil

2 tablespoons fresh lemon juice

1 teaspoon dried oregano

½ teaspoon grated lemon rind

½ teaspoon crumbled dried rosemary

½ teaspoon salt

½ teaspoon pepper

4 (1-inch-thick) swordfish steaks (about 1½ pounds)

1 Mix olive oil, lemon juice, oregano, lemon rind, rosemary, salt, and pepper in a resealable plastic bag. Add fish steaks; toss to coat. Marinate at room temperature 30 minutes, turning occasionally.

2 Prepare a medium grill or heat broiler. Cook steaks about 5 minutes per side for medium doneness.

TUNA, NOODLE, AND BROCCOLI BAKE

PER SERVING
Net Carbs: 7 grams
Total Carbs: 11.5 grams
Fiber: 4.5 grams

Protein: 25.5 grams
Fat: 28 grams
Calories: 384

Servings: 6
Prep time: 20 minutes
Bake/cook time: 50 minutes

This traditional favorite is made with low carb pasta and broccoli for color and texture. If you like, crumble low carb soy chips over the casserole before baking.

2 tablespoons butter, plus extra to grease baking dish

1½ cups Atkins Quick Quisine™ Pasta Cuts, any small cut

½ bunch broccoli, cut into small florets (about 2½ cups)

1 (12-ounce) can solid white tuna, packed in water or oil, drained and coarsely flaked

1 small onion, finely chopped

1½ cups heavy cream

½ cup water

1½ tablespoons ThickenThin™ Not Starch thickener

¼ teaspoon salt

¼ teaspoon pepper

1 Butter a shallow 2-quart baking dish; set aside. Heat oven to 400° F.

2 Cook pasta according to package directions, drain, and rinse under cold water. Transfer to a large bowl and set side.

3 Cook broccoli in lightly salted boiling water 5 minutes, until crisp-tender. Drain and rinse under cold water. Mix in with pasta. Add tuna and toss gently.

4 Melt 2 tablespoons butter in a medium saucepan over medium heat. Add onion and cook about 7 minutes, stirring occasionally, until soft. Stir in the cream, water, thickener, salt, and pepper, and cook 5 to 8 minutes, until mixture boils and thickens.

5 Pour sauce over pasta mixture and toss to combine. Transfer to prepared baking dish. Bake 20 to 30 minutes, until top is nicely browned and casserole is bubbly. Let cool slightly before serving.

MUSSELS WITH WHITE WINE AND GARLIC

PER SERVING

3 4 | **Net Carbs: 13.5 grams** | Protein: 40.5 grams | Servings: 4
| Total Carbs: 13.5 grams | Fat: 10.5 grams | Prep time: 5 minutes
| Fiber: 0 grams | Calories: 361 | Cook time: 10 minutes

If you are in Induction or OWL, have a half portion as an appetizer. You can vary the broth by adding a bit of cream at the end of the cooking time.

3 pounds mussels

1 cup dry white wine

2 cloves garlic, finely chopped

2 tablespoons chopped fresh Italian (flat-leaf) parsley

1 tablespoon butter or olive oil

1 Wash mussels thoroughly and remove the beards (the string-like appendages sticking out from the shells) by gripping them with a dry kitchen towel and pulling straight out.

2 Mix wine, garlic, parsley, and butter in a 5-quart pot with a tight-fitting lid. Bring to a quick simmer, add the mussels, and cover tightly. Steam for 10 minutes, or until shells open; discard any unopened mussels. Divide mussels and broth in soup bowls.

SALMON FILLETS WITH CUCUMBER RIBBONS

PER SERVING

Net Carbs: 1 gram
Total Carbs: 1 gram
Fiber: 0 grams

Protein: 45.5 grams
Fat: 36 grams
Calories: 520

Servings: 4
Prep time: 10 minutes
Cook time: 12 minutes

This recipe balances the rich texture of salmon with the lightness of cucumbers seasoned with a splash of tarragon vinegar. English cucumbers are usually quite large—choose the smallest ones you can find.

2 small English cucumbers, peeled and halved crosswise

1 teaspoon salt, divided

1 tablespoon butter

2½ tablespoons olive oil, divided

4 (2-inch-thick) center-cut salmon fillets (about 2 pounds)

½ teaspoon pepper, divided

½ packet sugar substitute

2 teaspoons tarragon vinegar

1 With a vegetable peeler, peel ribbons along the length of each cucumber half. Keep going until you reach the center core of seeds; discard core. In a bowl, toss cucumber ribbons with ½ teaspoon salt; set aside.

2 In a large skillet over medium-high heat, melt butter in 1 tablespoon oil. Season fish with ½ teaspoon salt and ¼ teaspoon pepper. Place fish flesh side down in skillet. Cook 10 minutes, turning carefully once halfway through cooking time, until golden brown and just cooked through. Remove from skillet and tent with foil.

3 Wipe out skillet with a paper towel. Heat remaining 1½ tablespoons oil over medium-high heat until oil shimmers. Add cucumber to skillet; sprinkle with remaining ¼ teaspoon pepper and sugar substitute. Cook about 2 minutes, stirring occasionally, until cucumber is just warmed through. Stir in vinegar. Divide cucumber on individual serving plates; top each with a piece of salmon.

SPICY TUNA STEAKS

PER SERVING

Net Carbs: 1 gram
Total Carbs: 1.5 grams
Fiber: 0.5 gram

Protein: 42 grams
Fat: 18 grams
Calories: 345

Servings: 4
Prep time: 10 minutes
Cook time: 4 minutes

Spice rubs eliminate marinating time. Before cooking, simply rub the seasoning directly on food to boost the flavor quotient. This particular mix is inspired by the cuisine of Thailand.

2 tablespoons grated lemon rind

2 teaspoons kosher salt

2 teaspoons ground coriander

1½ teaspoons freshly ground pepper, plus more to taste

1½ teaspoons ground ginger

½ teaspoon ground cinnamon

4 tablespoons olive oil, divided

4 (1-inch-thick) tuna steaks (about 1½ pounds)

2 cups baby greens (mesclun)

1 teaspoon balsamic vinegar

Salt and pepper

1 In a small bowl, combine lemon rind, salt, coriander, 1½ teaspoons pepper, ginger, and cinnamon. Stir in 2 tablespoons oil; mix well. Rub mixture onto tuna steaks.

2 Heat 1 tablespoon oil in a large skillet over high heat until it shimmers. Add tuna steaks and cook 4 minutes, turning once halfway through cooking time, until seared. If you prefer your fish more well done, increase cooking time 1 to 2 minutes per side.

3 While fish is cooking, toss greens with vinegar and remaining tablespoon of olive oil. Add salt and pepper to taste. To serve, cut fish into ¼-inch slices and place on greens.

WARM SCALLOP SALAD

PER SERVING
Net Carbs: 11 grams
Total Carbs: 12.5 grams
Fiber: 1.5 grams

3 4

Protein: 29.5 grams
Fat: 8 grams
Calories: 246

Servings: 4
Prep time: 10 minutes
Cook time: 5 minutes

When purchasing scallops, avoid those that are stark white, which indicates that they have been soaked in water to increase their weight. Soaked scallops tend to release a lot of water when cooked, so it's worthwhile finding a fish store that sells cream-colored or pearl-pink scallops.

1½ pounds sea scallops, patted dry

¾ teaspoon salt, divided

2 tablespoons olive oil, divided

1½ cups diced red bell pepper

½ cup corn kernels

½ cup sliced green onion

2 tablespoons fresh lime juice

2 tablespoons chopped fresh cilantro

Orange slices, for garnish (optional)

1 Toss scallops with ½ teaspoon of the salt. In a 12-inch nonstick skillet, heat 1 tablespoon oil over high heat until very hot. Add scallops in a single layer, flat side down. Cook 2 minutes, without moving, until golden; turn and cook 2 minutes more. With a slotted spoon, transfer scallops to a large bowl.

2 Reduce heat slightly and add remaining tablespoon of oil, bell pepper, and corn. Cook 1 minute and add to bowl with scallops. Stir in green onion, lime juice, cilantro, and remaining salt.

3 To serve, arrange overlapping orange slices (if using) on a plate and spoon salad on top.

BEEF, PORK, VEAL, & LAMB

Spices, condiments, and herbs make simple protein foods like beef, pork, and lamb— all staples of the Atkins lifestyle—interesting and flavorful. Broiled lamb chops are good, but wait until you try our Indian-Spiced Lamb Chops! Borrowing from cuisines from Asia to Italy, these recipes are straightforward and diverse.

INDIAN-SPICED LAMB CHOPS WITH SPINACH

PER SERVING
Net Carbs: 4 grams
Total Carbs: 9 grams
Fiber: 5 grams

Protein: 66 grams
Fat: 41 grams
Calories: 669

Servings: 4
Prep time: 5 minutes
Cook time: 10 minutes

In this recipe the lamb chops are seared for a deep brown crust and then cooked in the oven for a tender texture. However, if you like, you may continue the cooking right in the skillet.

2 tablespoons curry powder

1¼ teaspoon salt, divided

½ teaspoon freshly ground pepper

¼ teaspoon ground cinnamon

8 lamb rib chops, or 4 (½-inch-thick) leg of lamb steaks (about ¾ pound each)

1 tablespoon canola oil

⅔ cup sour cream

1 small garlic clove, pushed through a press

2 (10-ounce) bags fresh spinach leaves, cooked

1 Heat oven to 350° F. Combine curry, 1 teaspoon salt, pepper, and cinnamon in a cup. Sprinkle each side of lamb chops with 1 teaspoon of the spice mixture.

2 Heat oil in a large skillet over medium-high heat; add 2 chops and cook 1½ minutes per side, just until deep brown. Transfer to broiler pan. Repeat browning process with the remaining 6 chops.

3 Bake chops 3 to 4 minutes, until just pink in center or to desired doneness.

4 Stir sour cream, garlic, and remaining salt into the hot spinach; serve with lamb chops.

ANCHO MACHO CHILI

PER SERVING
Net Carbs: 3 grams
Total Carbs: 6 grams
Fiber: 3 grams

Protein: 58.5 grams
Fat: 40 grams
Calories: 644

Servings: 8
Prep time: 10 minutes
Cook time: 2 hours 45 minutes

For a more distinctive flavor, use McCormick's® ancho chile pepper or Mexican-style chili powder (from the company's gourmet line of spices). Jarred roasted garlic cloves can be found in well-stocked supermarkets.

5 pounds boneless beef chuck stew meat

2 teaspoons kosher salt

½ teaspoon freshly ground pepper

2 tablespoons olive oil or vegetable oil, divided

1 medium onion, chopped

3 tablespoons ancho chile pepper powder or Mexican-style chili powder

1 (14½-ounce) can diced tomatoes with green chiles

¾ cup dry red wine or chicken broth

4 large roasted garlic cloves, minced

1 Heat oven to 325° F. Toss beef with salt and pepper. Heat 1½ teaspoons oil in a Dutch oven over high heat. Add one-third of the beef and brown on all sides, about 5 minutes. Transfer to a bowl and repeat two more times with beef and oil.

2 Add the last 1½ teaspoons oil to Dutch oven and cook onion until lightly browned. Stir in chile powder, tomatoes, wine, and garlic; bring to a simmer. Return beef and accumulated juices to Dutch oven. Cover and bake 2½ hours, stirring once halfway through cooking time, until beef is very tender.

CHILI-RUBBED HAM STEAK WITH ZUCCHINI SALSA

PER SERVING
Net Carbs: 6 grams

Total Carbs: 9.5 grams
Fiber: 3.5 grams

Protein: 47 grams
Fat: 16 grams
Calories: 378

Servings: 4
Prep time: 15 minutes
Cook time: 12 minutes

You'd be hard-pressed to find an easier weeknight meal. If you prefer your salsa mild, seed and devein the jalepeño before chopping.

SALSA:

1 zucchini, cut into ½-inch dice

½ cup canned black beans, rinsed and drained

2 tablespoons fresh lime juice

1 tablespoon extra-virgin olive oil

¼ teaspoon salt

¼ medium onion, finely chopped

1 small jalapeño pepper, minced

HAM:

2 teaspoons olive or canola oil

1 thick-cut ham steak (about 2 pounds)

1 tablespoon chili powder

2 tablespoons no-sugar-added apricot jam,
    at room temperature or slightly warmed

1 Toss all salsa ingredients in a bowl.

2 Heat oil in a large skillet over medium-high heat. Sprinkle ham on both sides with chili. Add ham to skillet and cook 5 to 6 minutes (reduce heat slightly if ham begins to get too dark). Turn and repeat, cooking until ham is hot in center. Top with jam, spreading to coat top. Serve with salsa.

CANNELLONI WITH MEAT AND MUSHROOMS

PER SERVING

Net Carbs: 5.5 grams
Total Carbs: 7.5 grams
Fiber: 2 grams

Protein: 32.5 grams
Fat: 25.5 grams
Calories: 385

Servings: 6
Prep time: 40 minutes
Bake time: 30 minutes

Instead of pasta, we use homemade low carb "crespelle" (Italian for crêpes) in this recipe. Use a tomato sauce with fewer than 5 grams of Net Carbs per half cup.

CRESPELLE:

½ cup Atkins Quick Quisine™ Pancake & Waffle Mix

⅔ cup heavy cream

⅓ cup water

2 large eggs

¼ teaspoon salt

Vegetable oil cooking spray

FILLING:

½ tablespoon olive oil

2 large boneless, skinless chicken breast halves
(10 to 12 ounces total), trimmed

Salt and pepper

1 small onion, finely chopped

6 medium mushrooms, finely chopped

½ pound lean ground beef sirloin or round

½ cup heavy cream

⅓ cup grated Parmesan cheese, plus more for serving

¼ cup chopped fresh parsley

1½ cups tomato sauce, divided

1 FOR CRESPELLE: In a blender, combine pancake mix, cream, water, eggs, and salt. Blend at high speed until smooth. Let stand 15 minutes.

2 Heat one or two 7- or 8-inch nonstick sauté pans over medium-high heat. Spray with vegetable oil cooking spray. For each crespelle, add about 2 tablespoons batter to a pan, swirling to coat bottom evenly. Cook 1 minute or until edges are brown, carefully loosen with a spatula, flip, and cook 30 seconds more. Cool crespelle in a single layer on kitchen towels.

3 FOR FILLING: Heat oil in a large heavy skillet over medium heat. Season chicken with salt and pepper. Cook chicken 5 minutes per side, until browned and cooked through. Transfer to a cutting board. Cool slightly, and finely chop with a large knife. Transfer to a bowl.

4 Add onion to the fat in the skillet and cook over medium heat, stirring occasionally, until softened, about 5 minutes. Add mushrooms and cook, stirring, 5 minutes more. Add ground beef, breaking up meat with a spatula, and cook about 5 minutes, until browned. Add beef mixture to bowl with chicken. Stir in cream, ⅓ cup Parmesan, parsley, and ¼ teaspoon each salt and pepper. Let cool completely.

5 Lightly butter a 9-inch by 13-inch baking dish. Add ½ cup tomato sauce to dish and tilt to coat bottom evenly; set aside.

6 Heat oven to 400° F. To make each cannelloni, scoop up ¼ cup of the filling and form into a cylinder with your hands. Place in the center of a crespelle. Fold 1 edge over the filling, flattening it slightly. Roll the crespelle over again, and place in the prepared dish, seam side down. Repeat with remaining crespelle and filling. They should fit snugly in the pan.

7 Spoon remaining cup of sauce over the cannelloni. Cover dish tightly with aluminum foil. Return to oven and bake 20 to 30 minutes, until hot and bubbly. Serve with additional Parmesan.

CHEDDAR BURGERS WITH CHIPOTLE SAUCE

PER SERVING
Net Carbs: 1 gram
Total Carbs: 1 gram
Fiber: 0 grams

Protein: 53 grams
Fat: 49.5 grams
Calories: 673

Servings: 4
Prep time: 10 minutes
Cook time: 10 minutes

Chipotles, smoked jalapeño peppers, add a great smoky heat to foods. This recipe makes four large burgers, but you can make six smaller ones instead.

2 pounds ground beef chuck

4 teaspoons Atkins Quick Quisine™ Steak Sauce

½ teaspoon salt

1 cup (4 ounces) shredded cheddar cheese

¼ cup mayonnaise

1 chipotle pepper en adobo, finely chopped

1 Prepare a medium grill or heat broiler. Combine ground beef, steak sauce, and salt. Form into 4 patties, about 1 inch thick and 3½ inches in diameter.

2 Grill patties, covered, 5 minutes per side for medium-rare doneness (cook longer, if desired). Two minutes before the burgers are done, top with cheddar cheese and cover grill.

3 While burgers are cooking, mix mayonnaise and chipotle. Top burgers with sauce and serve.

FRUIT-GLAZED PORK OVER MIXED GREENS

PER SERVING

Net Carbs: 3 grams
Total Carbs: 3.5 grams
Fiber: 0.5 gram

Protein: 48 grams
Fat: 20.5 grams
Calories: 412

Servings: 6
Prep time: 10 minutes
Bake time: 25 minutes

The delicious glaze does double duty: It gives the pork a fruity crust and is the base for a tasty salad dressing. If you can't find marmalade without added sugar, simply use more of the apricot jam.

4 (12-ounce) pork tenderloins

1¼ teaspoons salt

½ teaspoon freshly ground pepper

5 tablespoons olive oil, divided

⅓ cup no-sugar-added orange marmalade

⅓ cup no-sugar-added apricot jam

½ teaspoon ground cinnamon

1 tablespoon plus 1½ teaspoons balsamic vinegar

1 garlic clove, pushed through a press

6 cups (5 ounces) mixed greens

1 Heat oven to 400° F. Season tenderloins with salt and pepper. In a large skillet over medium high, heat 1 tablespoon of the oil. Brown pork for about 10 minutes, turning as needed. Transfer to a rimmed baking sheet and place in oven.

2 Roast pork for 10 minutes. Meanwhile, in a small bowl, whisk together orange marmalade, apricot jam, and cinnamon. Transfer 1 tablespoon of the jam mixture to a large bowl and set aside.

3 Brush pork with jam mixture. Cook 5 minutes more or until just cooked through and a meat thermometer registers 160° F. Transfer pork to a cutting board and let stand for 5 minutes before cutting into 1-inch diagonal slices.

4 Whisk the vinegar, garlic, and the remaining oil into the reserved jam mixture. Add greens and toss to coat. Divide greens on plates and top with pork slices and any accumulated juices.

SAVORY APRICOT BRISKET

PER SERVING
Net Carbs: 0.5 gram
Total Carbs: 0.5 gram
Fiber: 0 grams

Protein: 47 grams
Fat: 16.5 grams
Calories: 355

Servings: 8
Prep time: 10 minutes
Bake time: 3 hours 30 minutes

This brisket is oven-baked until very tender, then spread with jam for a succulent glaze. Don't fret about the carbohydrates in the carrots and onions—they're used just to flavor the cooking liquid.

1 (4-pound) beef brisket

2 teaspoons kosher salt

2 teaspoons paprika

1 teaspoon freshly ground pepper

4 onions, quartered lengthwise

8 carrots, cut into 2-inch pieces

½ cup water

3 tablespoons no-sugar-added apricot jam

1 Heat oven to 475° F. Season brisket with salt, paprika, and pepper. Place brisket fat side down in a Dutch oven. Scatter onions and carrots around the beef. Cook 15 minutes. Turn brisket fat side up and add ½ cup water. Cover tightly. Reduce oven temperature to 375° F. Cook 3 hours, or until brisket is fork tender.

2 Heat broiler. Remove brisket from Dutch oven and place on a broiler pan. Spread jam over brisket. Broil 6 inches from heat source 5 minutes, until jam is lightly browned in spots. While brisket is broiling, remove onions and carrots from cooking juices and discard. Tilt Dutch oven and remove surface fat with a spoon.

3 Let brisket rest 15 minutes before carving. Serve with degreased cooking juices.

BARBECUED HAM

PER SERVING
Net Carbs: 1.5 grams
Total Carbs: 2 grams
Fiber: 0.5 gram

Protein: 33.5 grams
Fat: 26.5 grams
Calories: 391

Servings: 10
Prep time: 25 minutes
Cook time: 1 hour 30 minutes

If you've never prepared ham this way, you are in for a treat. Grilling is handy at holiday time because it frees up oven space, and indirect grilling (cooking food next to, rather than directly over, the heat source) is largely unattended.

1 tablespoon chili powder

1 tablespoon paprika

1 teaspoon ground cumin

½ teaspoon ground cinnamon

¼ teaspoon ground cloves

2 packets sugar substitute

1 (6- to 7-pound) fully cooked bone-in smoked ham, shank or butt portion

⅓ cup no-sugar-added apricot jam

1 Prepare the grill for indirect heat. Place a disposable aluminum drip pan in center of bottom grate or floor of grill. For a closed gas grill, heat on high for 10 to 15 minutes, then turn off heat source directly under pan, leaving the other one or two burners on. Adjust heat to register between 375° F and 425° F on an oven thermometer. For a charcoal grill, build two equal piles of briquettes on either side of drip pan. Burn coals about 25 minutes, until they are covered with gray ash.

2 Meanwhile, combine chili powder, paprika, cumin, cinnamon, cloves, and sugar substitute in a cup. Score top and sides of ham with a sharp knife in a crisscross pattern. Sprinkle rub over all sides.

3 Place ham on prepared grill over pan. Close lid and grill 45 minutes. Turn ham over (adding more briquettes if necessary), and grill 45 to 60 minutes more, until an instant-read thermometer inserted in center of ham (away from bone) registers 140° F.

4 Spoon or brush jam over ham. Cover and grill 5 minutes more. Let stand 15 minutes before carving.

FUSILLI ALLA BOLOGNESE

PER SERVING

Net Carbs: 15.5 grams
Total Carbs: 27.5 grams
Fiber: 12 grams

Protein: 51.5 grams
Fat: 26.5 grams
Calories: 564

Servings: 4
Prep time: 20 minutes
Cook time: 2 hours (largely
unattended)

Long, slow cooking is the hallmark of Bolognese sauce. This recipe uses chopped, not ground, beef. You may do this at home, or ask your butcher to do it for you.

1 tablespoon olive oil

1 small onion, coarsely chopped

2 carrots, grated

1 rib celery, finely chopped

½ pound chopped beef

⅓ cup red wine

¼ cup beef stock or water

1 ½ cups canned chopped tomatoes with their juice

½ teaspoon salt

¼ teaspoon freshly ground pepper

½ cup heavy cream

8 ounces Atkins Quick Quisine™ Pasta Cuts, fusilli shape

Parmesan cheese (optional)

1 In a large saucepan, heat olive oil over medium-high heat. Add onion, carrots, and celery and cook until tender, about 10 minutes.

2 Add chopped beef, breaking it up with a wooden spoon. Cook about 7 minutes, until no longer pink. Add wine, stock, tomatoes, salt, and pepper. Bring to a boil. Reduce heat; simmer 1 ½ hours, stirring occasionally, until about three-quarters of the liquid has evaporated. Add heavy cream and cook 2 minutes, to warm through.

3 During the last 20 minutes of sauce cooking time, prepare pasta according to package directions. Drain pasta and toss with sauce. Top with shaved Parmesan, if using.

BUTTERFLIED LEG OF LAMB

PER SERVING

Net Carbs: 1.5 grams
Total Carbs: 2.5 grams
Fiber: 1 gram

Protein: 43 grams
Fat: 12 grams
Calories: 300

Servings: 8
Prep time: 10 minutes
Bake time: 1 hour

This impressive entrée is a lot easier to make than it looks. Once your butcher has butterflied the lamb, all you need to do is prepare a simple coating and pop the whole thing in the oven.

1 ½ slices Atkins Bakery™ Ready-to-Eat
  Sliced White Bread

1 butterflied leg of lamb (about 3 ½ pounds trimmed,
  5 pounds untrimmed)

1 teaspoon salt

½ teaspoon freshly ground pepper

1 teaspoon chopped fresh rosemary

¼ cup Dijon mustard

2 garlic cloves, chopped

⅓ cup chopped fresh parsley

1 Heat oven to 200° F. Place bread in oven for 15 minutes, or until dried but not browned. Raise oven temperature to 375° F. Place bread in a food processor and process into fine crumbs.

2 Rub lamb with salt, pepper, and rosemary. Place lamb in a roasting pan and spread mustard over lamb. In a small bowl, combine breadcrumbs, garlic, and parsley. Gently pat crumb mixture over lamb.

3 Cook 45 minutes, or until internal temperature reaches 135° F on an instant-read thermometer for medium-rare. Let rest 15 minutes before carving.

Atkins Tip: An instant-read thermometer is important to accurately judge when the lamb is ready.

GRILLED FENNEL, SAUSAGE, AND TOMATO PASTA

PER SERVING
Net Carbs: 11 grams
Total Carbs: 23 grams
Fiber: 12 grams

Protein: 53.5 grams
Fat: 30 grams
Calories: 645

Servings: 4
Prep time: 20 minutes
Cook time: 25 minutes

3 4

Italian sausage contains fennel seed, which has a piquant licorice flavor. This recipe combines a brightly flavored sauce, cooked fennel, and tomato.

1 large beefsteak tomato (about 1 pound), chopped

1 small fennel bulb, cored, bulb cut into ¼-inch slices, stalks thinly sliced

3 tablespoons olive oil, divided

1 tablespoon balsamic vinegar

¾ teaspoon salt, divided

⅜ teaspoon freshly ground pepper, divided

12 ounces of Atkins Quick Quisine™ Pasta Cuts, penne shape

1¼ pounds Italian sausage, sweet or hot

1 Heat grill to medium. In a large bowl, toss tomato, fennel stalks, 2 tablespoons of the oil, vinegar, ½ teaspoon salt, and ¼ teaspoon pepper. Set aside while pasta cooks.

2 Prepare pasta according to package directions. Drain; return to pasta pot and toss with tomato mixture.

3 Brush fennel bulb slices with remaining 1 tablespoon oil and season with remaining salt and pepper. Grill or broil fennel and sausage about 10 minutes, turning as needed, until fennel is fork-tender and sausage is cooked through.

4 Slice sausage into ½-inch rounds. Coarsely chop fennel. Add sausage and fennel to pasta mixture and gently toss to mix. Serve hot or at room temperature.

ROAST BEEF WITH HORSERADISH CRUST

PER SERVING

Net Carbs: 3.5 grams
Total Carbs: 6 grams
Fiber: 2.5 grams

Protein: 80 grams
Fat: 48 grams
Calories: 795

Servings: 6
Prep time: 15 minutes
Cook time: 1 hour 25 minutes
(largely unattended)

This cut of beef also goes by the names of tri-corner, center rump, or center bottom. Dijon mustard gives the classic combination of roast beef and horseradish extra zing.

3 slices Atkins Bakery™ Ready-to-Eat Sliced White Bread

1 tablespoon olive oil

2 teaspoons dried tarragon

4½-pound beef rump roast

4 garlic cloves, cut in large slices

1 teaspoon salt

½ teaspoon pepper

¼ cup Dijon mustard

2 tablespoons prepared horseradish

1 Heat oven to 225° F. Bake bread on oven rack 15 minutes, until dried out. Place in food processor fitted with a steel blade. Process in pulses until coarse crumbs form. Toss crumbs with oil and tarragon.

2 Increase oven temperature to 450° F. With tip of small knife, make the same number of incisions as garlic slices all over meat surface. Insert one slice in each incision. Place roast on jelly-roll pan. Season meat with salt and pepper.

3 Mix mustard and horseradish; slather over all sides of roast, except the bottom and front face. Pat seasoned crumbs onto mustard.

4 Roast 10 minutes, until crumbs are browned. Lightly tent with aluminum foil. Reduce heat to 350° F and roast about 1 hour 15 minutes more until internal temperature registers 120° F on a meat thermometer (for rare doneness; if you prefer medium-done beef, let temperature reach 135° F). Remove from oven and let meat rest 15 to 30 minutes before thinly slicing. Remove and discard garlic pieces as they fall.

FLANK STEAK WITH SOUTHWESTERN RUB

PER SERVING

Net Carbs: 1.5 grams
Total Carbs: 3 grams
Fiber: 1.5 grams

Protein: 60 grams
Fat: 29.5 grams
Calories: 529

Servings: 2
Prep time: 5 minutes
Cook time: 8 minutes

If you want a "beefier" taste to your meat, substitute a skirt steak or hanger steak for the milder-tasting flank.

2 garlic cloves

½ teaspoon salt

1½ teaspoons chili powder

1 teaspoon ground cumin

¼ teaspoon cayenne pepper

¼ teaspoon ground cinnamon

1½ teaspoons grated lime rind

1 tablespoon olive oil

1¼-pound flank steak

2 tablespoons chopped fresh cilantro

1 Heat broiler. Mash garlic and salt with side of knife to make a paste. In small bowl combine garlic paste, chili powder, cumin, cayenne, and cinnamon. Add lime rind and olive oil, mixing to combine. Coat meat with rub.

2 Broil 8 minutes, turning once, for medium rare. Sprinkle with cilantro. Slice thinly; serve warm with accumulated juices poured over meat.

GRILLED ASIAN PORK PATTIES

PER SERVING
Net Carbs: 3.5 grams
Total Carbs: 3.5 grams
Fiber: 0 grams

Protein: 41.5 grams
Fat: 38 grams
Calories: 525

Servings: 4
Prep time: 15 minutes
Cook time: 12 minutes

Pork patties are a nice change of pace, and these are both tender and flavorful.
The teriyaki-flavored dipping sauce is the perfect accompaniment.

PATTIES:

2 pounds ground pork

¼ cup Atkins Quick Quisine™ Teriyaki Sauce

¼ cup green onions, white and green parts chopped

1 tablespoon chopped peeled fresh ginger

2 teaspoons chopped garlic

SAUCE:

¼ cup Atkins Quick Quisine™ Teriyaki Sauce

1 tablespoon chopped green onion, white and
green parts

2 teaspoons dark sesame oil

1 teaspoon chopped peeled fresh ginger

1 teaspoon chopped garlic

1 FOR PATTIES: Prepare a medium grill or heat broiler.
Combine ground pork, teriyaki sauce, green onions,
ginger, and garlic. Form into 6 patties, a little less than
½ inch thick.

2 FOR SAUCE: Combine teriyaki sauce, green onion,
sesame oil, ginger, and garlic.

3 Grill patties, covered, 6 to 7 minutes per side until just
cooked through. Serve with sauce.

ITALIAN-STYLE STEAK AND ZUCCHINI

PER SERVING
Net Carbs: 3 grams
Total Carbs: 4 grams
Fiber: 1 gram

Protein: 45.5 grams
Fat: 40 grams
Calories: 567

Servings: 4
Prep time: 15 minutes
Cook time: 15 minutes

Boneless sirloin makes a more tender quick steak than round, which is typically used
for minute steak. If you can't find a thin cut of sirloin, cut the steak horizontally with
a sharp knife to make it one-quarter inch thick and omit the pounding.

2 pounds boneless sirloin steak, no more than
½ inch thick

2 large garlic cloves

1¼ teaspoons salt, divided

½ teaspoon freshly ground pepper

1 tablespoon plus 1 teaspoon olive oil

1 large zucchini, cut in half lengthwise and sliced into
half-moons

1 tablespoon sun-dried tomato pesto

1 Cut steak into 4 even pieces. Pound each with a meat
pounder or rolling pin to flatten to about ¼ inch thick.
Finely chop garlic with 1 teaspoon of the salt on a
cutting board to form a paste. Rub paste on to both
sides of steaks and sprinkle evenly with pepper.

2 Heat 1 tablespoon of the olive oil in a large nonstick skillet
over medium-high heat. Add zucchini and cook 5 to
8 minutes; turn slices as they brown. Sprinkle with the
remaining ¼ teaspoon salt and fold in pesto; transfer to
plate. Wipe out skillet.

3 Heat remaining 1 teaspoon olive oil in skillet over
high heat. Add steaks and cook 1 to 1½ minutes per
side, until browned for medium-rare or longer if
desired. Serve immediately with zucchini.

GRILLED STEAK OVER SALAD

PER SERVING

Net Carbs: 5.5 grams
Total Carbs: 6.5 grams
Fiber: 1 gram

Protein: 55 grams
Fat: 43 grams
Calories: 639

Servings: 4
Prep time: 10 minutes
Cook time: 14 minutes

Fennel is a vegetable you should get to know. It has a mild licorice flavor and a crisp and refreshing texture when served raw. Cooked, it becomes mild and sweet. If you aren't partial to the flavor of fennel, substitute thinly sliced celery.

STEAKS:

4 (8- to 10-ounce) beef rib-eye steaks

Salt and pepper

6 cups baby greens (mesclun)

1⅓ cups fennel bulb, shaved (see Tip)

DRESSING:

6 tablespoons extra-virgin olive oil

2 tablespoons Dijon mustard

1 tablespoon fresh lemon juice

Salt and freshly ground pepper to taste

1 Prepare grill or heat broiler. Sprinkle steaks with salt and pepper. Grill over high heat 8 to 10 minutes for rare, 12 to 14 minutes for medium doneness, turning once.

2 FOR DRESSING: In a bowl, whisk together olive oil, mustard, and lemon juice. Add salt and pepper to taste. Set aside.

3 In a large bowl, mix greens and fennel; toss with dressing. Divide salad on plates. Thinly slice steak and fan out over salads.

Atkins Tip: Use a vegetable peeler to shave the white portion (root) of the fennel. The green fronds can be used as garnish.

STUFFED VEAL BREAST

PER SERVING
Net Carbs: 10 grams

3 4

Total Carbs: 15 grams
Fiber: 5 grams

Protein: 75 grams
Fat: 76.5 grams
Calories: 1,059

Servings: 8
Prep time: 30 minutes
Bake time: 3 hours (largely unattended)

The spinach and mushroom stuffing can be made a day ahead. To save time, ask your butcher to cut a pocket in the veal and trim most of the fat (but not all—fat keeps the meat moist).

¼ cup olive oil

1 cup pecans, coarsely chopped

¾ cup finely chopped shallots

2 pounds mushrooms (a mixture of white, shiitake, cremini, and/or portabello), sliced

1 tablespoon plus 1 teaspoon salt

1 teaspoon pepper, divided

1½ pounds baby spinach, rinsed and dried

1 sheet matzo or 6 water crackers

1 veal breast, about 7 pounds, trimmed and slit horizontally to form a pocket for stuffing

1 Heat oven to 350° F. Heat 2 tablespoons olive oil over high heat. Add pecans; cook, stirring, until fragrant, about 1 minute. Add shallots; cook 4 minutes, stirring occasionally until softened. Add half the mushrooms; cook 5 minutes, stirring occasionally, until most of the liquid has evaporated. Transfer mixture to a large bowl.

2 Heat remaining 2 tablespoons oil over high heat. Add remaining mushrooms, 1 teaspoon salt, and ½ teaspoon pepper. Cook 5 minutes. Add one-third of the spinach at a time, adding a new batch as it wilts. Drain, reserving liquid. Add mushroom mixture to bowl.

3 Run the matzo under warm water to soften. Crumble into bowl with mushroom mixture; mix well.

4 Sprinkle meat, including pocket, with remaining 1 tablespoon salt and ½ teaspoon pepper. Place veal in a roasting pan. Fill cavity with about 2 cups of stuffing. Close pocket; secure with skewers. Place remaining stuffing in 9-inch square baking pan, cover with foil; set aside. Put reserved cooking liquid in the roasting pan. Cover with foil. Cook 2½ hours, until almost fork-tender.

5 Remove foil and increase heat to 450° F. Place pan of stuffing in oven. Cook veal until browned on top and fork-tender, about 30 minutes. Cool 15 minutes before slicing. If desired, reduce the cooking liquid by half, skim off fat, and serve as gravy.

VIETNAMESE PORK STIR-FRY

PER SERVING

Net Carbs: 7 grams
Total Carbs: 8.5 grams
Fiber: 1.5 grams

Protein: 47 grams
Fat: 29 grams
Calories: 495

Servings: 4
Prep time: 15 minutes
Cook time: 10 minutes

Chili sauce is a fiery mix of chiles, onions, peppers, and spices. We used a full tablespoon, but if you prefer food on the milder side, reduce the amount by half.

1 (2-pound) center-cut pork loin roast, cut into ¼-inch by 2-inch-long strips

3 large garlic cloves, pushed through a press

2 teaspoons grated peeled fresh ginger

⅓ cup reduced-sodium chicken broth

1 tablespoon Asian hot chili sauce

2 teaspoons Asian fish sauce (nam pla)

¼ packet sugar substitute

5 teaspoons dark sesame oil, divided

½ pound shiitake mushrooms, stems discarded, sliced

1 onion, cut into thin wedges

⅓ cup fresh basil leaves, thinly sliced

1 In a bowl, toss pork strips with garlic and ginger until coated. Combine broth, chili sauce, fish sauce, and sugar substitute in a cup.

2 Heat 2 teaspoons sesame oil in a large nonstick skillet over high heat. Add half the pork and cook 1½ minutes without stirring, until browned. Turn and repeat. Remove. Repeat with 2 teaspoons oil and remaining pork.

3 Heat remaining teaspoon oil in same skillet, add mushrooms and onion, cover, and cook 2 minutes. Uncover and cook about 3 minutes more, until lightly browned. Add all pork, sauce, and basil to skillet and heat through, stirring, 2 minutes.

PORTERHOUSE WITH MUSHROOM TOPPING

PER SERVING

Net Carbs: 4.5 grams
Total Carbs: 6 grams
Fiber: 1.5 grams

Protein: 44 grams
Fat: 33.5 grams
Calories: 505

Servings: 4
Prep time: 10 minutes
Cook time: 15 minutes

Any thinly sliced mushroom can be substituted for the white mushrooms. Try oyster, cremini, or baby bellas for subtle taste variations.

4 porterhouse steaks

1 teaspoon salt, divided

½ teaspoon ground pepper, divided

3 tablespoons butter, divided

2 tablespoons olive oil

2 large shallots, chopped

1 pound white mushrooms, sliced

1 Heat broiler. Season steaks with ½ teaspoon salt and ¼ teaspoon pepper.

2 In large skillet over medium high heat, melt 2 tablespoons of the butter in the olive oil. Add the shallots and cook 2 to 3 minutes, stirring until translucent. Add mushrooms and remaining salt and pepper. Cook, stirring occasionally, about 7 minutes, until most of the mushroom liquid has been given off. Add remaining 1 tablespoon butter; stir to combine.

3 Meanwhile, broil steaks 12 minutes, turning once during cooking time, for medium-rare doneness. Serve steaks smothered with mushrooms and accumulated juices.

STEAK WITH SPINACH AND BLUE CHEESE

PER SERVING

Net Carbs: 2.5 grams
Total Carbs: 6.5 grams
Fiber: 4 grams

Protein: 54.5 grams
Fat: 49 grams
Calories: 683

Servings: 4
Prep time: 10 minutes
Cook time: 30 minutes

Well-dried spinach works best to make a creamy sauce. To save time, purchase triple-washed packaged spinach.

2 large cloves garlic

1 teaspoon salt

¼ teaspoon pepper

1 (2-pound) boneless sirloin steak (about 1½ to
    1¾ inch thick)

1½ teaspoons olive or canola oil

1 tablespoon butter

2 (10-ounce) bags spinach leaves

4 ounces Maytag Blue cheese, crumbled

1 Heat oven to 425° F. Chop the garlic, salt, and pepper together on a board until a paste forms; rub evenly on both sides of steak.

2 Heat oil in a large ovenproof skillet over high heat. Add the steak and cook 3 minutes per side, until deeply browned; transfer to oven and roast 15 to 20 minutes for medium-rare or longer for more doneness. Let stand 10 minutes.

3 During stand time, melt butter in a large saucepan over medium heat. Add spinach and cover with a tight-fitting lid. Cook 1 minute, until spinach wilts. Add cheese and stir to melt. Divide spinach on plates. Cut steak into ¼-inch thick slices; lay slices over spinach and drizzle with drippings.

PORK WITH SALSA VERDE

PER SERVING

Net Carbs: 1.5 grams
Total Carbs: 2.5 grams
Fiber: 1 gram

Protein: 48.5 grams
Fat: 20 grams
Calories: 397

Servings: 6
Prep time: 10 minutes
Cook time: 12 minutes

The salsa verde in this recipe is used in two ways: as a seasoning, and as a sauce. If using wooden skewers, soak them in water for one hour before using so they won't burn.

12 (12-inch) skewers

SALSA VERDE:

2 cups lightly packed fresh cilantro leaves

1 cup fresh flat-leaf parsley

¼ cup chopped onion

2 garlic cloves

⅓ cup extra-virgin olive oil, divided

2 tablespoons white wine vinegar

1 tablespoon water

PORK:

2 large pork tenderloins (3 pounds total)

1½ teaspoons kosher or 1 tablespoon regular salt

1 FOR SALSA: Place cilantro, parsley, onion, and garlic in a food processor and process until finely chopped. Add the oil, vinegar, and water; process until thick.

2 FOR PORK: Heat grill to medium-high. Cut tenderloins in half lengthwise, then crosswise into 1-inch slices (you should have about 48 kebob chunks). Toss with salt on a cutting board. Thread 4 chunks of pork onto each of 12 skewers. Transfer one-third of the salsa verde to a cup (reserve remaining sauce) and brush onto pork.

3 Grill pork covered 6 minutes per side, until lightly charred in spots and cooked through. Serve with reserved salsa verde.

MUSHROOM-FLAVORED MEATLOAF

PER SERVING

Net Carbs: 3 grams
Total Carbs: 5 grams
Fiber: 2 grams

Protein: 35 grams
Fat: 23 grams
Calories: 380

Servings: 6
Prep time: 10 minutes
Bake time: 1 hour

Mushrooms add moistness and flavor to this savory loaf. Leftover meatloaf makes great sandwiches, so plan ahead!

2 slices Atkins Bakery™ Ready-to-Eat Sliced White Bread

1 tablespoon olive oil

2 cups sliced button mushrooms

1 teaspoon salt

1 large clove garlic

2 pounds ground beef

½ of 1 medium onion, grated or minced

1 large egg

2 tablespoons spicy brown mustard

½ teaspoon freshly ground pepper

1 Heat oven to 350° F. Line a broiler pan bottom or baking sheet with foil or parchment. Pulse bread in a food processor until crumbs form and set aside.

2 Heat oil in 12-inch skillet over high heat. Add the mushrooms; cook 8 to 9 minutes, stirring once or twice, until well browned. Sprinkle with salt and add garlic; cook 30 to 60 seconds more, until aromatic. Chop by hand or in food processor until very finely minced.

3 In a large bowl, gently combine meat with mushrooms and remaining ingredients until mixed. Form a 9-inch by 4-inch oblong loaf on prepared pan; cover with foil and bake 30 minutes. Uncover and bake 30 to 35 minutes more, until browned and an instant-read thermometer inserted into center of loaf registers 160° F.

Pasta with Roasted Vegetables and Ricotta, page 134

VEGETARIAN ENTRÉES

With the advent of low carb tortillas and pasta—in conjunction with traditional ingredients such as tofu and beans—new possibilities have arisen in vegetarian cooking, as recipes for Black Bean Tostadas or Pasta with Roasted Vegetables and Ricotta illustrate. Although a bit higher in carbs than most protein-based entrées, these dishes showcase just how versatile Atkins can be.

PASTA WITH ROASTED VEGETABLES AND RICOTTA

PER SERVING

`3 4`

Net Carbs: 14.5 grams
Total Carbs: 27.5 grams
Fiber: 13 grams

Protein: 45.5 grams
Fat: 26.5 grams
Calories: 519

Servings: 4
Prep time: 25 minutes
Cook time: 20 minutes

Chopped fresh herbs and two kinds of cheese perk up the flavor in this simple, homey vegetarian entrée.

½ cup whole-milk ricotta cheese

½ cup basil leaves, chopped

⅓ cup mint leaves, chopped

¾ teaspoon salt, divided

1 large zucchini (about 8 ounces), diced

2 yellow squash (about 12 ounces total), diced

1 large red bell pepper, quartered lengthwise, sliced

¼ cup olive oil, preferably extra-virgin

3 large garlic cloves, pushed through a press

½ teaspoon freshly ground pepper

8 ounces Atkins Quick Quisine™ Pasta Cuts, fusilli shape

¼ cup oil-packed sun-dried tomatoes, finely chopped

½ cup grated Asiago or Parmesan cheese

1 Heat oven to 450° F. In small bowl, combine ricotta, basil, mint, and ¼ teaspoon salt. Set aside.

2 In large shallow roasting pan, toss zucchini, yellow squash, bell pepper, oil, garlic, pepper, and remaining ½ teaspoon salt. Spread out. Bake 15 to 20 minutes, stirring once, or until tender.

3 Prepare pasta according to package directions. Reserve ⅓ cup pasta cooking water; drain pasta.

4 Add sun-dried tomatoes and reserved cooking water to roast vegetables; stir to combine. Divide hot pasta among plates. Sprinkle with half of the Asiago. Top each serving with vegetables and a spoonful of ricotta mixture in the center. Serve remaining Asiago on the side.

PASTA WITH BASIL AND FETA CHEESE

PER SERVING

`3 4`

Net Carbs: 16.5 grams
Total Carbs: 33.5 grams
Fiber: 17 grams

Protein: 70 grams
Fat: 44 grams
Calories: 792

Servings: 2
Prep time: 10 minutes
Cook time: 10 minutes

Greek feta cheese is better known, but French fetas tend to be creamier in texture and a little less salty. Both types are delicious—it's a matter of personal preference. This recipe serves two as an entrée or four as a side dish.

8 ounces Atkins Quick Quisine™ Pasta Cuts, fusilli shape

2 tablespoons olive oil, divided

1 cup cherry or grape tomatoes, halved

½ teaspoon salt

¼ teaspoon freshly ground pepper

1 tablespoon fresh lemon juice

1 teaspoon grated lemon rind

½ cup black olives, halved and pitted

4 ounces mushrooms, thinly sliced

½ cup loosely packed basil, chopped

3 green onions, green and white parts thinly sliced

4 ounces feta cheese, crumbled

1 Prepare pasta according to package directions. Reserve ½ cup pasta cooking water and drain the rest. Transfer pasta to a large bowl and toss with 1 tablespoon of the oil.

2 While pasta is cooking, toss tomatoes, salt, pepper, remaining oil, lemon juice, and lemon rind in a bowl to combine. Set aside.

3 When pasta is at room temperature, add reserved tomato mixture, olives, mushrooms, basil, green onions, feta, and reserved pasta water, ¼ cup at a time, if needed, gently tossing to combine. Serve at room temperature.

AVOCADO-TOMATO QUESADILLAS

PER SERVING
Net Carbs: 13 grams

3 4

Total Carbs: 25.5 grams
Fiber: 12.5 grams

Protein: 22 grams
Fat: 31grams
Calories: 428

Servings: 4
Prep time: 15 minutes
Cook time: 10 minutes

A layer of mashed seasoned beans topped with zesty rich cheese makes these quesadillas a good source of fiber and protein.

½ cup canned pink beans, drained and rinsed

¾ teaspoon chili powder

½ teaspoon grated lime rind

2 tablespoons olive oil, divided

1 teaspoon water

2 medium tomatoes, seeded and chopped (about 1 cup)

2 tablespoons chopped red onion

2 tablespoons chopped fresh cilantro

8 ounces (2 cups) Pepper Jack cheese, shredded

4 low carb tortillas, any flavor

½ avocado, cut into 8 slices

1 In a food processor fitted with a steel blade, pulse beans, powder, and rind to combine. With machine running, add 1 tablespoon oil and 1 teaspoon water. Scrape down sides as needed. Process until a smooth paste forms.

2 Combine tomatoes, red onion, and cilantro in a bowl. Stir in cheese.

3 Heat ½ tablespoon oil in a large nonstick skillet over medium-high heat. Fry 2 tortillas 30 seconds to 1 minute, until golden brown spots appear on undersides. Place on paper towel, uncooked side up.

4 Spread 2 rounded tablespoons of bean mixture on half of each tortilla. Top with ¾ cup salsa mixture and two slices of avocado. Fold tortillas in half over filling. Place back in skillet. Cover and cook 30 seconds on medium-low heat to melt cheese. Repeat with remaining tortillas and fillings.

GREEN BEANS AND TOFU WITH PEANUT SAUCE

PER SERVING
Net Carbs: 10.5 grams
Total Carbs: 16 grams
Fiber: 5.5 grams

Protein: 19 grams
Fat: 34 grams
Calories: 419

Servings: 4
Prep time: 15 minutes
Cook time: 15 minutes

3 4

Tofu needs to be dried very well to allow it to brown and avoid splattering when cooked. Place slices between paper towels to absorb excess moisture.

¼ cup plus 1 tablespoon peanut oil, divided

1 pound extra-firm tofu, drained and sliced lengthwise into 8 (¼-inch-thick) planks

1 pound green beans, trimmed

¾ cup water, divided

¾ teaspoon salt, divided

½ chopped peeled fresh ginger

2 cloves garlic, pushed through a press

⅛ to ¼ teaspoon red pepper flakes

¼ cup plus 1 tablespoon unsweetened peanut butter

1 tablespoon low-sodium soy sauce

½ teaspoon sugar substitute

2 tablespoon chopped toasted peanuts (optional)

Dark sesame oil (optional)

1 Heat ¼ cup oil in large nonstick skillet over medium-high heat until it shimmers. Add tofu; cook about 6 minutes, until golden brown, turning once. Remove from pan and drain on paper towels.

2 In same skillet, add beans; cook 3 minutes, stirring occasionally, until bright green and flecked with golden brown spots. Add ¼ cup water and cover loosely with aluminum foil. Continue to cook 3 to 4 minutes until water has evaporated and beans are crisp-tender. Season with ½ teaspoon salt. Remove beans from pan and reserve.

3 Reduce heat to medium. Add remaining tablespoon oil and heat until it shimmers. Add ginger, garlic, and red pepper; stir about 30 seconds, until fragrant. Add peanut butter, ½ cup water, soy sauce, sugar substitute, and remaining ¼ teaspoon salt. Cook and stir 1 minute, until sauce is combined. Return green beans to skillet and toss to coat with sauce.

4 To serve, divide the beans on plates and top with overlapping tofu slices. Sprinkle with chopped salted peanuts and a drizzle of sesame oil, if desired.

KALE, TOMATO, AND BEAN STEW

PER SERVING

`3` `4`

Net Carbs: 16.5 grams
Total Carbs: 26 grams
Fiber: 9.5 grams

Protein: 8.5 grams
Fat: 8 grams
Calories: 195

Servings: 4
Prep time: 15 minutes
Cook time: 22 minutes

Fire-roasted tomatoes are extra flavorful—roasting brings out the tomatoes' natural sweetness. If there are any leftovers, just add to broth for a tasty soup or mix with low carb pasta.

2 tablespoons olive oil

4 garlic cloves, thinly sliced

½ teaspoon dried rosemary

2 pounds kale, tough stems removed, leaves washed and cut into 2-inch pieces

1 cup water

1 cup crushed tomatoes, preferably fire-roasted

½ teaspoon salt

¼ teaspoon pepper

1 cup canned white beans, rinsed and drained

Parmesan cheese (optional)

1 In a large saucepan over medium-high heat, heat olive oil until it shimmers. Add garlic and rosemary. Cook, stirring, about 1 minute, until garlic turns golden brown.

2 Add kale and 1 cup water. Cover the pan and cook 5 minutes, stirring occasionally, until kale has reduced to about 2 cups and is tender.

3 Stir in tomatoes, salt, pepper, and beans. Reduce heat to low and cook 15 minutes for flavors to blend. Serve with shavings of Parmesan cheese, if desired.

CHEF SALAD WITH GORGONZOLA DRESSING

PER SERVING

Net Carbs: 7 grams
Total Carbs: 14 grams
Fiber: 7 grams

Protein: 21 grams
Fat: 41.5 grams
Calories: 500

Servings: 4
Prep time: 45 minutes

Not your ordinary Chef Salad: This contains protein-rich tempeh, a densely textured soy food, and a splash of rice wine vinegar.

DRESSING:

¼ cup mayonnaise

¼ cup sour cream

⅓ cup crumbled Gorgonzola cheese

2 tablespoons water

Salt and pepper to taste

SALAD:

2 cups sliced mushrooms

2 tablespoons unseasoned rice vinegar

Salt and pepper to taste

5 tablespoons olive oil, divided

1 (8-ounce) package garden veggie tempeh, cut into ¼-inch-thick slices (such as Lightlife brand)

8 cups cut-up Romaine lettuce

1 cup shredded red cabbage

1 kirby cucumber, thinly sliced

6 radishes, sliced

1 cup grape or cherry tomatoes, halved

4 hard-boiled eggs, peeled and quartered

1 FOR DRESSING: In small bowl, stir mayonnaise, sour cream, Gorgonzola cheese, water, and salt and pepper to taste until blended; cover and refrigerate.

2 FOR SALAD: In bowl, combine mushrooms, vinegar, salt, and pepper to taste, and 1 tablespoon oil; toss and set aside.

3 In a large skillet, heat remaining 4 tablespoons oil over medium heat. Add tempeh in batches and cook 3 minutes per side, until browned. Remove to paper towels.

4 On plates, arrange lettuce, cabbage, cucumber, radishes, tomatoes, eggs, marinated mushrooms, and tempeh. Serve with dressing on the side.

EGGPLANT ROLLATINI

PER SERVING
Net Carbs: 10 grams
Total Carbs: 15 grams
Fiber: 5 grams

Protein: 22 grams
Fat: 34.5 grams
Calories: 484

Servings: 6
Prep time: 20 minutes
Bake/cook time: 40 minutes

This Italian classic can be made ahead and frozen. If baking from a frozen state, increase bake time by fifteen minutes.

4 small eggplants (about 6 ounces each), trimmed and sliced ⅛ to ¼ inch thick (24 slices)

Salt

1½ cups water

¾ cup Atkins Quick Quisine™ Bake Mix

2 eggs, lightly beaten

Olive oil for frying

Butter for greasing pan

1¼ cups low carb tomato sauce (such as Rao's)

FILLING:

2 cups whole-milk ricotta cheese

4 ounces mozzarella cheese, shredded

2 eggs

⅓ cup finely grated Parmesan cheese

¼ cup finely chopped fresh parsley

¼ teaspoon salt

¼ teaspoon pepper

1 Arrange eggplant slices in layers in a colander, sprinkling each layer lightly with salt. Let stand 15 minutes for bitter juices to drain, then rinse and pat dry.

2 In a large bowl, whisk together water, bake mix, and 2 eggs until smooth.

3 Heat about ¼ cup olive oil in a heavy large skillet over medium-high heat until hot but not smoking. Dip eggplant, one slice at a time, in the batter, then add to the skillet. Cook eggplant in batches (slices should not touch), turning occasionally, 5 to 6 minutes, until tender and golden. Use more oil as necessary. Drain eggplant on paper towels; cool on sheets of wax paper.

4 Heat oven to 400°F. Lightly butter a 9-inch by 13-inch baking pan. Add ½ cup tomato sauce and tilt pan to coat.

5 FOR FILLING: In a large bowl, mix ricotta, mozzarella, eggs, Parmesan, parsley, salt, and pepper with a wooden spoon until well blended. Place a heaping tablespoon of filling in the center of each eggplant slice and roll up. Place rolls seam side down in prepared pan, arranging in rows. Spoon remaining tomato sauce on top of rolls.

6 Cover pan with foil; bake 30 minutes. Remove foil and bake 10 minutes, until bubbly and lightly browned.

STUFFED PORTABELLO STACKS

PER SERVING
Net Carbs: 11 grams
Total Carbs: 16.5 grams
Fiber: 5.5 grams

Protein: 15 grams
Fat: 18 grams
Calories: 276

Servings: 4
Prep time: 20 minutes
Bake time: 25 minutes

The surprise ingredient in this hearty entrée is a layer of garlic-flavored hummus.

4 large portabello mushrooms (about 1 pound), stems discarded

2 tablespoons olive oil, divided

Salt and pepper

1 bunch Swiss chard (1 pound), stems removed, cut into 2-inch pieces

½ cup garlic-flavored hummus

¼ cup grated Parmesan cheese

2 plum tomatoes, thinly sliced

1 cup mozzarella cheese, shredded

1 Heat oven to 400° F. With a teaspoon scrape away undersides of mushrooms to remove dark brown gills. Brush lightly with some of the oil; season with salt and pepper. Place mushrooms gill side down on a rimmed baking sheet. Bake 10 minutes, or until tender; set aside.

2 In a large skillet, heat remaining oil over medium heat. Add chard and cook, stirring frequently, 5 minutes, or until tender and any liquid evaporates.

3 Turn mushrooms over and spread with hummus. Top with chard; sprinkle with Parmesan cheese. Top with tomatoes and sprinkle with mozzarella cheese.

4 Bake 10 minutes, or until cheese is melted and bubbly.

BLACK BEAN TOSTADAS

PER SERVING

Net Carbs: 11.5 grams
Total Carbs: 25.5 grams
Fiber: 14 grams

Protein: 16.5 grams
Fat: 21.5 grams
Calories: 326

Servings: 4
Prep time: 30 minutes
Bake time: 10 minutes

High in fiber, iron, and protein, legumes are one of the first foods you should add as you get close to your goal weight.

SAUCE:

¼ cup sour cream

2 tablespoons chopped fresh cilantro

1 tablespoon fresh lime juice

2 teaspoons water

¼ to ½ teaspoon Tabasco® sauce

Salt and pepper to taste

TOSTADAS:

4 low carb tortillas, any flavor

1 tablespoon olive oil

1 teaspoon chili powder or ground cumin

2 cups finely shredded Romaine lettuce

¾ cup canned black beans, rinsed and drained

4 ounces Pepper Jack cheese, diced

1 small tomato, diced

½ avocado, peeled, diced

2 green onions, sliced

1 FOR SAUCE: In a bowl, combine ingredients. Set aside.

2 FOR TOSTADAS: Heat oven to 400° F. Brush tortillas on both sides with olive oil and place on a cookie sheet. Sprinkle with chili powder. Bake 10 minutes, or until browned in spots. Set aside.

3 In a bowl, toss lettuce, beans, cheese, tomato, avocado, and green onions. Place tortillas on plates, top with salad, and drizzle with sauce.

OPEN-FACED ROAST VEGGIE MELTS

PER SERVING

Net Carbs: 10 grams
Total Carbs: 18.5 grams
Fiber: 8.5 grams

Protein: 25.5 grams
Fat: 37 grams
Calories: 489

Servings: 4
Prep time: 25 minutes
Bake time: 25 minutes

Roasting vegetables brings out their sweetness and flavor. Pimiento-stuffed olives and fresh basil make this vegetarian sandwich extra flavorful.

1 zucchini (about 10 ounces), cut into ½-inch-thick slices

1 small red bell pepper, cut into ½-inch-wide strips

1 small red onion, sliced (about ½ cup)

1 tablespoon olive oil

Salt and pepper

¼ cup cream cheese

½ cup loosely packed fresh basil leaves, chopped

8 pimiento-stuffed green olives, finely chopped

4 slices Atkins Bakery™ Ready-to-Eat Sliced Bread, lightly toasted

1 small tomato, sliced

8 ounces fontina or Monterey Jack cheese, sliced

1 avocado, halved, pitted, peeled, and sliced

½ cup alfalfa sprouts

1 Heat oven to 450° F. On a large baking sheet, toss zucchini, bell pepper, onion, and oil. Sprinkle with salt and pepper to taste. Spread out to a single layer. Bake 15 to 20 minutes, or until vegetables are tender; set aside.

2 Meanwhile, in a small bowl, stir cream cheese, basil, and olives until blended. Spread one side of bread slices with cream-cheese mixture. Top with roasted vegetables. Transfer to a baking sheet. Top with tomato slices and fontina cheese.

3 Bake sandwiches 4 to 5 minutes, or until cheese melts. Top with avocado slices and sprouts.

ASIAN VEGETABLE NOODLES

PER SERVING
Net Carbs: 15.5 grams
Total Carbs: 28 grams
Fiber: 14 grams

3 4

Protein: 47 grams
Fat: 15.5 grams
Calories: 429

Servings: 4
Prep time: 30 minutes
Cook time: 12 minutes

The veggies in this dish are flavorful, colorful, varied in texture, and low in carbs. Feel free to substitute your own favorites. Have all your vegetables prepared before you start to cook the pasta.

12 ounces Atkins Quick Quisine™ Pasta Cuts, fettuccine shape

2 tablespoons dark sesame oil, divided

2 tablespoons vegetable oil

2 tablespoons chopped peeled fresh ginger

3 tablespoons chopped garlic

6 ounces oyster mushrooms, sliced

½ red bell pepper, chopped

2 medium carrots, cut into matchsticks

1 large head bok choy (about 1 pound), stems thinly sliced, leaves torn into small pieces

⅓ cup Atkins Quick Quisine™ Teriyaki Sauce

2 tablespoons soy sauce

2 tablespoons finely chopped green onions (optional)

2 tablespoons chopped peanuts (optional)

1 Prepare pasta according to package directions. Reserve ¼ cup pasta cooking water and drain the rest. Transfer pasta to a large bowl and toss with 1 tablespoon of the sesame oil. Cover lightly with plastic wrap.

2 In pasta pot, heat vegetable oil on high until it shimmers. Add ginger and garlic and cook, stirring, 30 seconds, until fragrant. Add mushrooms; cook 1 minute more. Add bell pepper; cook 1 minute more. Add carrots and bok choy stems; cook 1 minute more (add 2 tablespoons reserved pasta water if necessary).

3 Remove pot from heat. Add bok choy leaves, teriyaki sauce, soy sauce, and remaining tablespoon sesame oil. Toss well to mix.

4 Divide pasta on plates. Make a depression in the center of each and mound with one-fourth of the vegetable mixture. Garnish with chopped green onions and peanuts, if desired.

PASTA WITH BROCCOLI, CAULIFLOWER, AND TOFU

PER SERVING
Net Carbs: 15 grams
Total Carbs: 19 grams
Fiber: 4 grams

3 4

Protein: 24.5 grams
Fat: 30 grams
Calories: 414

Servings: 4
Prep time: 10 minutes
Cook time: 10 minutes

Red pepper flakes and a generous amount of garlic make this simple pasta dinner something special.

8 ounces Atkins Quick Quisine™ Pasta Cuts, penne shape

2 cups broccoli florets

2 cups cauliflower florets

3 tablespoons olive oil

3 large garlic cloves, pushed through a press

¼ teaspoon red pepper flakes

1 (8-ounce) package baked tofu, cut into ¾-inch cubes

½ cup grated Romano cheese

1 Prepare penne according to package directions. Add broccoli and cauliflower during last 4 minutes of cooking time. Reserve ½ cup pasta cooking water. Drain pasta and vegetables.

2 In same pot, heat oil, garlic, and red pepper over low heat, stirring constantly, until garlic is golden. Add tofu and cook 1 minute, or until hot. Add pasta and reserved cooking water; toss to combine. Remove pot from heat. Add cheese and toss; serve immediately.

LASAGNE

PER SERVING
Net Carbs: 10.5 grams
Total Carbs: 14.5 grams
Fiber: 4 grams

Protein: 35.5 grams
Fat: 37 grams
Calories: 529

Servings: 8
Prep time: 30 minutes
Cook time: 45 minutes

To make this "lasagne" we used eggplant and portabello mushroom layers instead of pasta. Though a bit time-consuming, the final result is well worth the effort.

2 medium Italian eggplants (about ¾ pound each)

1 pound ground beef round

1 cup spicy tomato sauce

4 medium portabello mushroom caps (about 12 ounces), stems discarded

¼ cup olive oil, divided

Salt and pepper

2 cups ricotta cheese

1 (10-ounce) box frozen leaf spinach, thawed and squeezed dry

2 eggs

¼ cup grated Parmesan cheese, plus more for serving

1 pound mozzarella cheese, sliced, divided

1 Trim the eggplants, discarding the stems and leaving peels on, then thinly slice lengthwise ¼ to ⅓ inch thick. Arrange in layers in a colander, sprinkling each layer with salt. Let stand in the sink 15 minutes for bitter juices to drain.

2 In a heavy medium skillet over medium heat, cook beef about 6 minutes, breaking up the meat with a wooden spoon, until browned and beginning to crisp. Drain liquid from skillet and stir in tomato sauce. Remove from heat; set aside to cool.

3 With a small sharp knife, scrape away the undersides of the mushrooms to remove the dark brown gills. Brush mushrooms lightly with some of the olive oil; season with salt and pepper. Cook mushrooms 4 minutes per side in a grill pan or large skillet over medium heat until lightly browned and tender. Cut into ½-inch-thick slices; set aside.

4 Heat broiler. Rinse eggplant slices and pat dry. Brush on both sides with olive oil and season with pepper. Broil 3 minutes per side until surface just begins to char; set aside to cool slightly. Reduce oven temperature to 400° F.

5 In a food processor fitted with a metal blade, combine ricotta, spinach, eggs, and Parmesan cheese, pulsing until blended. Season to taste with pepper.

6 Lightly oil a 9-inch by 13-inch glass baking dish. Arrange half of the eggplant slices in an even layer on the bottom, overlapping slightly. Top with half of the mozzarella and all of the mushrooms. Spoon half of the meat sauce on top, then add the ricotta mixture, spreading in an even layer. Arrange the remaining eggplant over the ricotta, then top with the remaining sauce and mozzarella.

7 Bake lasagne about 20 minutes, until the cheese is melted and the sauce is bubbly. Let cool slightly before cutting and serving.

MU SHU VEGGIE WRAPS

PER SERVING

Net Carbs: 8.5 grams
Total Carbs: 19.5 grams
Fiber: 11 grams

Protein: 14.5 grams
Fat: 16.5 grams
Calories: 253

Servings: 4
Prep time: 25 minutes
Cook time: 10 minutes

When you crave authentic Chinese food, try this winning recipe. Made with low carb tortillas, it makes a quick weeknight meal.

1 tablespoon olive oil, divided

4 large eggs, beaten

2 green onions, thinly sliced

Salt and pepper

¼ pound shiitake mushrooms, stems discarded, caps thinly sliced

2 cups coleslaw mix (cabbage and carrots)

¼ cup chopped red bell pepper

¼ cup Atkins Quick Quisine™ Teriyaki Sauce

¼ cup chopped peanuts

4 low carb whole-wheat tortillas, heated

1 In a large nonstick skillet, heat half of the oil over medium heat. In a bowl, combine eggs, green onions, and salt and pepper to taste. Add to skillet and cook 2 minutes, stirring frequently, until eggs are scrambled. Turn eggs out onto a plate; set aside.

2 Add remaining oil to skillet and increase heat to medium-high. Sauté mushrooms 3 minutes, or until tender and any liquid evaporates. Add coleslaw mix and bell pepper; sauté 2 minutes, or until cabbage is tender-crisp. Stir in teriyaki sauce and peanuts. Remove skillet from heat and stir in eggs. Spoon mixture onto tortillas and roll up.

Italian Ricotta Cheesecake, page 146

DESSERTS & SWEETS

Thanks to low carb sweeteners, soy flours, and thickeners, you can delight in all manner of decadent meal-enders. From dense, fudgey chocolate cake to creamy custards to refreshing fruit ices—there are countless ways to satisfy your sweet tooth without sabotaging your weight-loss goals. Sugar-, flour-, and cornstarch-free, these recipes prove that low carb baking has never been better. But remember: A single serving will do!

ITALIAN RICOTTA CHEESECAKE

PER SERVING
Net Carbs: 8 grams
Total Carbs: 9 grams
Fiber: 1 gram

Protein: 18 grams
Fat: 27.5 grams
Calories: 349

Servings: 10
Prep time: 15 minutes
Bake time: 1 hour 10 minutes
Chill time: 30 minutes

Baking in a water bath gives this cheesecake a creamy texture and ensures even cooking. Simply place a large roasting pan in the center rack of the oven, put the cheesecake pan in the middle, and fill with enough hot water to come at least halfway up the sides of the pan.

CRUST:

1½ cups finely ground walnuts or pecans

2 tablespoons melted butter

½ teaspoon ground cinnamon

FILLING:

2 pounds ricotta cheese

4 ounces cream cheese, softened

4 eggs

1½ cups granular sugar substitute

3 tablespoons Atkins Quick Quisine™ Bake Mix

1 tablespoon vanilla extract

2 teaspoons grated lemon rind

1 Heat oven to 350° F. Line the outside of an 8-inch springform pan with a double layer of aluminum foil. Combine crust ingredients; pat onto bottom and sides of pan. Bake 10 to12 minutes, until golden; cool on a wire rack.

2 In a food processor fitted with a metal blade, process ricotta until very smooth. Add cream cheese; process until smooth. Add eggs, one at a time, processing until incorporated. Add sugar substitute, bake mix, vanilla, and lemon rind. Process until smooth, scraping down sides as needed. Pour filling into cooled crust; smooth top.

3 Bake cheesecake in a water bath 1 hour, until puffed and golden and a toothpick inserted 1 inch from the center comes out clean. Cool in oven 30 minutes. Remove from oven, cool to room temperature on a wire rack, then refrigerate until well chilled.

ALMOND FLAN

PER SERVING
Net Carbs: 3.5 grams
Total Carbs: 3.5 grams
Fiber: 0 grams

Protein: 4.5 grams
Fat: 26.5 grams
Calories: 269

Servings: 6
Prep time: 10 minutes
Bake time: 30 minutes
Chill time: 3 hours

If you aren't partial to the flavor of almonds, omit the almond extract and the nuts and use a tablespoon of vanilla extract instead.

3 egg yolks

2 eggs

1½ cups heavy cream

1 cup water

8 packets sugar substitute

1 teaspoon almond extract

Vegetable cooking spray

2 tablespoons chopped almonds

1 Heat oven to 350° F. Place a roasting pan on the center shelf in oven and fill almost halfway with boiling water. In a blender, combine yolks, eggs, cream, water, sugar substitute, and almond extract until very smooth. Pour through a sieve into a shallow 1-quart baking dish.

2 Carefully place dish in roasting pan (water should come halfway up sides). Bake 30 to 35 minutes, until a knife inserted in the center comes out clean. Transfer to a wire rack; cool to room temperature. Spray a piece of plastic wrap with cooking spray, lay directly over flan, and chill 3 hours in refrigerator. Garnish with chopped almonds.

CINNAMON FLAN CUPS

PER SERVING

Net Carbs: 2.5 grams
Total Carbs: 2.5 grams
Fiber: 0 grams

Protein: 4 grams
Fat: 20 grams
Calories: 265

Servings: 4
Prep time: 5 minutes
Bake/cook time: 1 hour
Chill time: 2 hours

Rich, creamy, and not too sweet, these individual desserts are a perfect finale to a Mexican meal. The flans are kept in their cups to simplify serving. If you wish, top each flan with an additional teaspoon or two of strained praline sauce.

1 cup heavy or whipping cream

⅔ cup water

3 tablespoons sugar-free praline sauce, strained

1 cinnamon stick

2 eggs

1 Heat oven to 325° F. In a small saucepan, bring cream, water, praline sauce, and cinnamon to a simmer. Remove from heat. Let stand 15 minutes; remove cinnamon stick.

2 In a medium bowl, beat eggs; gradually whisk in about one-third of the cream mixture. Return egg-cream mixture to the saucepan and whisk again briefly.

3 Pour mixture through a sieve into four 6-ounce ramekins or custard cups. Place cups in a large roasting pan; carefully pour enough boiling water into pan to reach halfway up sides of cups. Cover entire pan with foil. Bake 40 minutes, until custards are set in centers. Let cups stand in pan at room temperature 15 minutes.

4 Remove cups and cover with plastic wrap (stretch plastic over cup edges to avoid touching surface of custards). Refrigerate 2 hours, or until cold.

Atkins Tip: Sugar-free praline sauce is available at www.atkins.com.

BITTERSWEET CHOCOLATE BROWNIE THINS

PER SERVING (2 COOKIES)
Net Carbs: 3 grams
Total Carbs: 4.5 grams
Fiber: 1.5 grams

Protein: 3 grams
Fat: 9 grams
Calories: 108

Servings: 12
Prep time: 20 minutes
Bake time: 5 minutes

Keep whole-wheat pastry flour in your refrigerator for making low carb treats. A small amount provides just enough gluten to give baked goods a chewy texture.

2 tablespoons whole-wheat pastry flour

2 tablespoons Atkins Quick Quisine™ Bake Mix

¼ teaspoon baking powder

3 ounces unsweetened baking chocolate, coarsely chopped

6 tablespoons heavy cream

2 tablespoons unsalted butter

2 large eggs, at room temperature

¾ cup granular sugar substitute

1 Heat oven to 375° F. Line a baking sheet with parchment paper or aluminum foil; set aside. In a bowl, whisk together pastry flour, bake mix, and baking powder.

2 In a microwave-safe bowl, melt chocolate, cream, and butter on 50 percent power 1½ to 2 minutes, until butter is melted and chocolate is softened. Let stand 5 minutes; stir until smooth.

3 With an electric mixer on medium speed, beat eggs and sugar substitute until light and fluffy. Gradually beat the slightly warm chocolate mixture into the egg mixture. Beat in flour mixture on low speed just until combined.

4 Drop slightly rounded measuring teaspoonfuls of dough onto prepared sheet. Bake 5½ to 6 minutes, until just set but soft on top. Transfer to a wire rack to cool completely. Store in an airtight container.

Atkins Tip: Whole-wheat pastry flour is available at www.kingarthurflour.com.

COEUR A LA CRÈME

PER SERVING
Net Carbs: 2 grams
Total Carbs: 2 grams
Fiber: 0 grams

Protein: 3 grams
Fat: 16 grams
Calories: 167

Servings: 6
Prep time: 15 minutes
Chill time: 24 hours

This rich classic French dessert, traditionally made in a large, heart-shaped mold, is usually served with a strawberry purée. Our version uses disposable muffin tins for easy portion control.

4 ounces cream cheese

¼ cup cottage cheese

¼ cup sour cream

½ cup heavy cream

2 packets sugar substitute

1 teaspoon vanilla extract

Pinch salt

1 Poke several holes in bottoms of disposable muffin tins. Wet a large square of cheesecloth, wring out, and fold in half. Drape cheesecloth over tin and press into molds, leaving a 2-inch overhang along border of tin.

2 In food processor, combine cream cheese, cottage cheese, and sour cream until smooth, scraping sides occasionally as needed; transfer to medium bowl.

3 With an electric beater, whip heavy cream, sugar substitute, vanilla, and salt in a bowl until stiff. In three additions, fold whipped cream into cheese mixture. Divide among tins; cover with overhanging cheesecloth.

4 Place tin on rack over baking sheet. Refrigerate 24 hours or until solid. To unmold, take cheesecloth off tops of molds and invert tin onto a platter. Remove tin and gently pull off cheesecloth. If desired, serve with strawberry purée, sweetened with sugar substitute.

COCONUT SAUCE

PER SERVING (4 TABLESPOONS)
Net Carbs: 2 grams
Total Carbs: 3 grams
Fiber: 1 gram

Protein: 1 gram
Fat: 13 grams
Calories: 125

Servings: 4
Cook time: 5 minutes

This dessert sauce is heavenly over low carb vanilla ice cream. Toasting the shredded coconut brings out its flavor and adds a lovely texture to the sauce.

¼ cup shredded unsweetened coconut

1 (5½-ounce) can unsweetened coconut milk

2 tablespoons sugar substitute

1 tablespoon heavy cream

½ teaspoon vanilla extract

1 Heat oven to 350° F. In a small pan, toast the coconut 5 minutes, until golden.

2 Meanwhile, in a bowl, whisk the coconut milk, sugar substitute, heavy cream, and vanilla together. Add the coconut, stirring until incorporated.

3 Serve chilled or at room temperature.

Atkins Tip: Unsweetened coconut is available in health food stores. Store in the freezer to maintain freshness.

CHOCOLATE SANDWICH COOKIES

PER SERVING (2 COOKIES)
Net Carbs: 7 grams
Total Carbs: 10 grams
Fiber: 3 grams

Protein: 3 grams
Fat: 16 grams
Calories: 176

Servings: 16
Prep time: 20 minutes
Chill time: 45 minutes
Bake time: 10 minutes

We filled these delicate cookies with raspberry filling, but choose any flavoring you like, including vanilla (just add 1 teaspoon of extract to the filling).

DOUGH:

2¼ cups granular sugar substitute

¼ cup soy flour

¼ cup whole-wheat pastry flour

¼ cup unsweetened cocoa powder

¼ teaspoon salt

8 ounces unsweetened chocolate, chopped

6 tablespoons unsalted butter

1½ teaspoons vanilla extract

2 large eggs

FILLING:

3 tablespoons unsalted butter, softened

1½ tablespoons no-sugar-added raspberry jam

1½ tablespoons cream cheese, softened

1 In a bowl, whisk together sugar substitute, soy flour, pastry flour, cocoa powder, and salt. In medium saucepan over low heat, melt chocolate and butter, stirring occasionally. Let cool. Whisk vanilla and eggs into chocolate mixture. Mix chocolate and flour mixtures until well combined.

2 Divide dough in half. Place each half on a sheet of plastic wrap or wax paper and form logs measuring 8 inches long and 1½ inches round. Roll up logs and chill at least 45 minutes.

3 Meanwhile, in a small bowl, beat butter, jam, and cream cheese until well blended; set aside.

4 Heat oven to 350° F. Cut dough logs into ¼-inch-thick slices and place on ungreased baking sheets ½ inch apart. Bake 10 minutes, until set. Place baking sheets on wire racks and let cookies cool completely.

5 Turn over half the cookies. Place about ½ teaspoon of filling on the surface of each bottom-side-up cookie. Top with remaining cookies, bottom-side-down.

Atkins Tip: To keep soft rolled dough logs round, insert them into empty paper-towel cardboard tubes before chilling.

APRICOT CLOUD

PER SERVING
Net Carbs: 10 grams
Total Carbs: 11.5 grams
Fiber: 1.5 grams

Protein: 1.5 grams
Fat: 22 grams
Calories: 247

Servings: 6
Prep time: 5 minutes
Chill time: 1 hour

Believe it or not, baby food is the secret in this creamy, indulgent dessert known in England as a "fool." For best texture, chill before serving.

1½ cups heavy cream

2 tablespoons granular sugar substitute

2 (8-ounce) jars no-sugar-added apricot baby food

1 Combine cream and sugar substitute in a medium bowl.

2 With an electric mixer on medium, beat cream and sugar substitute until soft peaks form. Fold in baby food.

3 Divide mixture among dessert glasses. Chill at least 1 hour.

CHEESE STRUDEL

PER SERVING

Net Carbs: 5 grams
3 4
Total Carbs: 5 grams
Fiber: 0 grams

Protein: 4.5 grams
Fat: 14 grams
Calories: 164

Servings: 12
Prep time: 20 minutes
Bake time: 40 minutes

Delicate phyllo sheets should be lightly covered with a damp towel to keep them pliable. If your supermarket doesn't carry whole-wheat phyllo, order it at www.fillofactory.com.

1 (8-ounce) package cream cheese, at room temperature

¼ cup granular sugar substitute

1 tablespoon ThickenThin™ Not Starch thickener

1 cup whole-milk ricotta cheese

1 large egg yolk

2 teaspoons freshly grated lemon rind

1½ teaspoons vanilla extract

4 sheets whole-wheat phyllo dough

4 tablespoons unsalted butter, melted

1 Heat oven to 400° F. In a large bowl, with an electric mixer on medium, beat cream cheese until smooth. Add sugar substitute; beat just until incorporated. Add thickener, ricotta, egg yolk, lemon rind, and vanilla. Beat until smooth, scraping down sides of bowl with a rubber spatula as needed.

2 Place an extra-wide sheet (or two overlapping sheets) of aluminum foil on a work surface. Lay a sheet of phyllo, long side parallel to you, on foil. Brush with butter. Repeat layering with remaining phyllo sheets, using all but 1 tablespoon of butter.

3 Spread cheese mixture over top third of phyllo surface, leaving a 1-inch border. Fold the long side of the phyllo dough border over cheese mixture, then fold the short sides over. Using the aluminum foil to help you, roll the phyllo log up toward you. Gently transfer log to a baking sheet.

4 Brush log with remaining butter. Bake about 40 minutes, or until golden brown. Cool on sheet 10 minutes; transfer to a wire rack to cool further. Serve warm or at room temperature.

FLOURLESS CHOCOLATE CAKE

PER SERVING

Net Carbs: 2.5 grams
Total Carbs: 3.5 grams
Fiber: 1 gram

Protein: 9 grams
Fat: 26 grams
Calories: 308

Servings: 8
Prep time: 25 minutes
Bake time: 25 minutes

Espresso powder complements the chocolate flavor in this luscious cake. If you prefer a milder flavor, omit the coffee and water.

8 Atkins Endulge™ Chocolate Candy Bars (plain or peanut), coarsely chopped

10 tablespoons unsalted butter

1 teaspoon instant decaffeinated espresso powder

1 tablespoon hot water

1 teaspoon vanilla extract

4 large eggs, at room temperature

1 Heat oven to 325° F. Grease an 8-inch round baking pan and line with parchment paper.

2 Melt chocolate and butter in a double boiler. Remove from heat and transfer to a large bowl. Mix espresso powder and water; stir into chocolate. Stir in vanilla extract. Set mixture aside to cool.

3 With an electric mixer on medium-high, beat eggs 6 minutes, until they fall in thick ribbons when beater is lifted. Stir one-third of the eggs into the chocolate mixture. In two additions, fold in remaining eggs. Pour batter into prepared pan; smooth top.

4 Bake 25 minutes, or until a toothpick inserted near middle of cake comes out with a few moist crumbs and cake is evenly raised. Cool completely on a wire rack.

5 To remove cake, run a knife around edge of pan. Dip bottom of pan into hot water for 1 minute, then turn cake out onto cutting board. Turn right side up onto a serving platter. Serve with whipped cream and grated chocolate curls, if desired.

EARL GREY—CHOCOLATE POTS DE CRÈME

PER SERVING
Net Carbs: 2.5 grams
Total Carbs: 7 grams
Fiber: 5 grams

Protein: 6 grams
Fat: 33 grams
Calories: 328

Servings: 4
Prep time: 15 minutes
Bake/cook time: 40 minutes
Chill time: 2 hours

Super silky in texture, with an intriguing, delicately sweet flavor, this baked custard is currently popular at many upscale restaurants. Earl Grey is a black tea made fragrant with bergamot oil.

1½ ounces unsweetened baking chocolate, coarsely chopped

1 cup heavy or whipping cream

⅔ cup water

3 Earl Grey tea bags

4 large egg yolks

5 tablespoons granular sugar substitute

Whipped cream, sweetened with sugar substitute (optional)

1 Heat oven to 325° F. Place chocolate in a small bowl. In a small saucepan over medium heat, bring cream and water to a simmer. Remove from heat. Pour just enough cream mixture over chocolate to cover (about ½ cup).

2 Add tea bags to remaining cream mixture in pan; steep 10 minutes. Squeeze tea bags over mixture; remove.

3 Whisk chocolate mixture until smooth. Whisk egg yolks and sugar substitute into the warm cream mixture in saucepan until well mixed, then whisk in the chocolate until smooth.

4 Pour mixture through a sieve into four 4-ounce ramekins or custard cups. Place cups in a large roasting pan. Place roasting pan in oven and carefully pour boiling water into pan until water comes halfway up sides of cups. Cover entire pan with foil and bake 33 to 35 minutes, until custards are set but slightly jiggly in center. Let stand in pan at room temperature 15 minutes.

5 Remove cups, cover with plastic wrap (stretch wrap over edges of cup so wrap does not touch custard), and refrigerate until cold. Serve topped with a dollop of whipped cream, if desired.

PAVLOVA WITH STRAWBERRIES

PER SERVING
Net Carbs: 6 grams
Total Carbs: 8 grams
Fiber: 2 grams

Protein: 4 grams
Fat: 3 grams
Calories: 75

Servings: 6
Prep time: 15 minutes
Bake time: 1 hour

A crisp meringue—named after a Russian ballerina—is the nest for strawberries. Be sure to let the meringue cool completely before filling with berries. Instead of Grand Marnier, you can substitute two tablespoons of sugar-free strawberry syrup.

6 egg whites, at room temperature

¼ teaspoon salt

¼ cup granular sugar substitute

½ cup pecans, coarsely chopped

1½ pints strawberries, halved

3 tablespoons Grand Marnier

1 Heat oven to 275° F. Cover a baking sheet with parchment and draw a 10-inch circle on it.

2 With an electric mixer on medium high, beat whites and salt in a bowl until stiff peaks form. Slowly add the sugar substitute, beating until very stiff, but not dry. Fold the pecans into the whites. Spread the meringue with a spatula or spoon to form a 10-inch nest on the parchment.

3 Bake about 1 hour, until lightly golden and a crust develops. Cool completely. Half an hour before serving, place strawberries in a bowl. Drizzle with Grand Marnier. To serve, arrange strawberries over the meringue shell.

LIME PANNA COTTA

PER SERVING
Net Carbs: 5.5 grams
Total Carbs: 5.5 grams
Fiber: 0 grams

Protein: 4 grams
Fat: 32 grams
Calories: 310

Servings: 6
Prep time: 15 minutes
Chill time: 4 hours

This version of panna cotta, Italian for "cooked cream," is true to the original with two significant differences. To cut carbs, we used sugar substitute and sugar-free hazelnut syrup. It takes fifteen minutes to whip up; the hard part is waiting for it to chill so you can revel in its tangy flavor and creamy texture!

Vegetable cooking spray

1 packet unflavored gelatin

¼ cup plus 3 tablespoons cold water

¼ cup Atkins™ Sugar Free Hazelnut Syrup

2 cups heavy cream

8 packets sugar substitute

1 tablespoon fresh lime juice

2 tablespoons grated lime rind

¼ cup shelled undyed pistachios

Lime rind strips for garnish

1 Spray six 6-ounce molds or dessert cups with cooking spray.

2 Sprinkle gelatin over 3 tablespoons of water in a small bowl. Let sit 5 minutes, until softened.

3 Meanwhile, in medium saucepan, combine hazelnut syrup, heavy cream, remaining ¼ cup water, sugar substitute, lime juice, and grated lime rind; bring to a boil over medium heat. Remove from heat; stir in gelatin mixture to melt.

4 Divide mixture among prepared molds. Cover with plastic wrap to prevent skin from forming. Refrigerate 4 hours or overnight.

5 Turn out molds onto serving plates, sprinkle with pistachios, and garnish with lime rind strips.

PINEAPPLE-COCONUT GRANITA

PER SERVING
Net Carbs: 8.5 grams
Total Carbs: 9.5 grams
Fiber: 1 gram

Protein: 0 grams
Fat: 0 grams
Calories: 29

Servings: 4
Prep time: 10 minutes
Cook time: 2 minutes
Chill time: 3 hours

This easy frozen dessert can be doubled or tripled as needed. Just make sure that the depth of the mixture is no more than a quarter-inch or it will not freeze properly.

½ pineapple, peeled and cored

1 cup water

½ cup granular sugar substitute

¾ teaspoon coconut extract

1 In a food processor fitted with a steel blade, purée the pineapple.

2 In a small saucepan, bring 1 cup water and the sugar substitute to a boil. Add to the pineapple. Stir in the coconut extract.

3 Pour mixture into a 9-inch by 13-inch pan. Place in freezer and freeze about 3 hours, until a hard slush forms, scraping with a fork to break up every 30 minutes.

FRESH FRUIT KEBOBS WITH ALMOND CRÈME

PER SERVING

Net Carbs: 12.5 grams

3 4

Total Carbs: 18 grams
Fiber: 5.5 grams

Protein: 3 grams
Fat: 7.5 grams
Calories: 147

Servings: 4
Prep time: 20 minutes

If you wish to prepare the kebobs ahead of time, place damp paper towels over them and cover tightly with plastic wrap. The accompanying yogurt dipping sauce is so good you'll find yourself inventing dishes to put it on!

8 (12-inch) skewers

KEBOBS:

2 kiwis (each cut into 4 rounds)

16 raspberries

16 blackberries

½ pint strawberries

1 star fruit, cut into 8 slices

ALMOND CRÈME:

¾ cup plain whole-milk yogurt

¼ cup heavy cream

1½ tablespoons granular sugar substitute

½ teaspoon almond extract

1 On each skewer thread 1 kiwi slice, 2 raspberries, 2 blackberries, 1 strawberry, and 1 star-fruit slice.

2 In a medium bowl, whisk yogurt, heavy cream, sugar substitute, and almond extract. Pour into serving dish. Serve kebobs with dipping sauce.

RASPBERRY CHEESECAKE IN A CUP

PER SERVING
Net Carbs: 5 grams
Total Carbs: 7 grams
Fiber: 2 grams

Protein: 8.5 grams
Fat: 33.5 grams
Calories: 358

Servings: 4
Prep time: 10 minutes
Bake time: 30 minutes
Chill time: 1 hour 30 minutes

Cream and raspberries are a culinary match made in heaven. Individual servings promote portion control.

CHEESECAKE:

8 ounces cream cheese, at room temperature

2 large eggs

½ cup heavy cream

3 packets sugar substitute

¼ teaspoon almond extract

¼ teaspoon freshly grated lemon rind

TOPPING:

½ pint fresh raspberries

3 tablespoons Atkins™ Sugar Free Raspberry Syrup

1 Heat oven to 325° F. Place four 6-ounce custard cups in a large roasting pan.

2 Process all cheesecake ingredients in a food processor until smooth, stopping when necessary to scrape down sides of processor.

3 Pour batter into cups. Add enough boiling water to roasting pan to come halfway up sides of cups. Cover with foil; bake 30 minutes. Turn oven off and let stand 20 minutes. Remove from oven, uncover, and cool completely. Cover cups with plastic wrap; transfer to refrigerator to chill.

4 When ready to serve, toss raspberries with syrup in a bowl. Sprinkle raspberries evenly over cheesecakes. Let stand at room temperature 15 minutes before serving for maximum creaminess.

DOUBLE CHOCOLATE–PECAN ICE CREAM

PER SERVING
Net Carbs: 6.5 grams
Total Carbs: 10.5 grams
Fiber: 4 grams

Protein: 7 grams
Fat: 46 grams
Calories: 477

Servings: 8
Prep time: 10 minutes
Cook time: 5 minutes
Chill time: 4 hours

It doesn't get any better than this: chocolate, pecans, and chocolate chunks!

1 teaspoon unflavored gelatin

1 cup water

6 egg yolks

16 packets sugar substitute

2½ cups heavy cream

⅔ cup unsweetened cocoa powder

1½ teaspoons vanilla extract

1½ teaspoons chocolate extract

1 cup toasted pecans, chopped

2 Atkins Endulge™ Chocolate Candy Bars, chopped

1 Sprinkle gelatin over water. Let stand until softened, about 5 minutes. In a medium bowl, whisk yolks and sugar substitute to combine.

2 In a medium saucepan, mix gelatin mixture and cream. Add cocoa powder. Cook over medium-low heat, stirring occasionally, until cocoa is dissolved and mixture has begun to simmer.

3 Slowly pour 1 cup of gelatin mixture into yolk mixture, whisking constantly. Pour mixture back into pan of gelatin mixture. Cook, stirring constantly, until mixture is thick enough to coat the back of a spoon. Remove from heat. Stir in vanilla and chocolate extracts. Chill mixture 4 hours.

4 Pour custard into ice cream maker. Freeze according to manufacturer's directions. About 5 minutes before ice cream is finished, add pecans and candy bars.

PEAR TART

PER SERVING
Net Carbs: 11.5 grams

`3 4`

Total Carbs: 14.5 grams
Fiber: 3 grams

Protein: 14.5 grams
Fat: 29.5 grams
Calories: 385

Servings: 6
Prep time: 40 minutes
Bake/cook time: 30 minutes

Choose pears that are just ripe—they should be slightly soft when pressed. Unless fruit is ripe, it will not soften properly during baking, and overripe fruit is difficult to slice thinly without bruising.

CRUST:

¾ cup Atkins Quick Quisine™ Bake Mix

4 tablespoons unsalted butter

3 ounces cream cheese

1 tablespoon sour cream

3 packets sugar substitute

FILLING:

2 small pears (Bartlett, Anjou, or Bosc), cored and thinly sliced lengthwise

⅓ cup plus 1 tablespoon sugar substitute, divided

2 tablespoons cognac or brandy

½ teaspoon almond extract, divided

½ teaspoon ground ginger

8 ounces cream cheese, at room temperature

1 egg

2 tablespoons no-sugar-added apricot jam

2 teaspoons hot water

2 tablespoons sliced almonds

1 FOR CRUST: Heat oven to 350° F. With an electric mixer on medium, beat bake mix, butter, cream cheese, sour cream, and sugar substitute until well combined. Pat dough on bottom and ½ inch up sides of a 10-inch tart pan. Prick dough with a fork and chill in freezer while preparing filling.

2 FOR FILLING: In a small bowl, toss pear slices with 1 tablespoon of the sugar substitute, the cognac, ¼ teaspoon of the almond extract, and the ginger until evenly distributed. Set aside. With the mixer, beat cream cheese until soft and creamy. Add remaining ⅓ cup sugar substitute; beat until smooth. Add egg and remaining ¼ teaspoon almond extract; beat until smooth. Scrape down sides of bowl as needed. Pour cream-cheese mixture into chilled tart shell.

3 Arrange pears on top of cream-cheese mixture in slightly overlapping concentric circles. If there is liquid left from the pears, pour it evenly over the tart. Bake 30 minutes, or until cheese mixture is just set. Remove from oven and place on a wire cooling rack.

4 Melt jam with 2 teaspoons hot water. Brush over hot tart and sprinkle with almonds. Let tart cool completely before serving.

RHUBARB-STRAWBERRY PIE

PER SERVING

Net Carbs: 7.5 grams
Total Carbs: 11.5 grams
Fiber: 4 grams

Protein: 4 grams
Fat: 24 grams
Calories: 298

Servings: 8
Prep time: 15 minutes
Bake time: 20 minutes
Chill time: 2 hours

3 4

Rhubarb is often paired with strawberries in a traditional springtime pie. But with frozen rhubarb and the year-round availability of strawberries, this pie can be enjoyed anytime.

One recipe Vanilla-Almond Butter Cookie dough (page 159)

4 stalks rhubarb (1¼ pounds), finely diced (4 cups)

½ cup water

4 packets sugar substitute

1 pint strawberries, hulled and quartered

1 tablespoon plus 2 teaspoons ThickenThin™ Not Starch thickener

½ teaspoon fresh lemon juice

⅛ teaspoon salt

1 cup heavy cream

1 teaspoon vanilla extract

1 Heat oven to 425° F. Pat dough into a pie plate; crimp edges. Chill in freezer 10 minutes. Prick all over with a fork. Bake 15 to 17 minutes until golden brown. Let cool completely before filling.

2 In a medium saucepan, combine rhubarb, water, and sugar substitute. Bring to a boil. Reduce the heat and simmer 10 minutes, until rhubarb is falling apart.

3 Stir in berries, thickener, lemon juice, and salt. Stir over low heat about 3 minutes, until thickened. Adjust sweetness by adding more sugar substitute, if desired. Let cool, stirring occasionally.

4 Pour filling into prepared pie shell. Chill until set, about 2 hours.

5 Before serving, whip the cream with vanilla until stiff peaks form. Pipe or spoon over the pie.

Atkins Tip: Allow enough time for the pie to set, at least 2 hours. Otherwise it will be too soft to slice.

STRAWBERRY-BANANA TRIFLE

PER SERVING
Net Carbs: 5.5 grams
Total Carbs: 14 grams
Fiber: 8.5 grams

Protein: 10 grams
Fat: 27 grams
Calories: 334

Servings: 12
Prep time: 20 minutes
Chill time: 1 hour

Originally trifles were created to use up cake that was slightly stale. Over the centuries, this British favorite has developed as a dessert in its own right. It is perfect for serving a crowd.

2 cups heavy cream

¾ cup granular sugar substitute, divided

4 teaspoons vanilla extract, divided

8 ounces cream cheese, melted and cooled

6 muffins made from Atkins Quick Quisine™ Banana Nut Bake Mix

¼ cup no-sugar-added apricot jam

1 pound strawberries, halved or quartered if large, divided

2 tablespoons sliced almonds, toasted

1 In a bowl, with an electric mixer on medium speed, beat cream, 2 tablespoons of the sugar substitute, and 2 teaspoons of the vanilla until soft peaks form. With a rubber spatula, fold two-thirds of the whipped cream into the cooled cream cheese; reserve remaining whipped cream. Whisk remaining 2 tablespoons sugar substitute and 2 teaspoons vanilla into cream-cheese mixture.

2 Cut muffins in thirds. Spread with apricot jam, then cut into 1-inch pieces.

3 To assemble: Spread one-third of the muffin pieces on the bottom of a 2-quart glass dessert dish; fit pieces together to cover the bottom of the dish. Spread half the cream-cheese mixture over muffin pieces; top with 1½ cups strawberries. Repeat layers. Scatter remaining muffin pieces over strawberries; cover berries with whipped cream. Scatter remaining berries and almonds over whipped cream. Chill 1 hour for flavors to blend.

VANILLA-ALMOND BUTTER COOKIES

PER SERVING (1 COOKIE)
Net Carbs: 4.5 grams
Total Carbs: 6 grams
Fiber: 1.5 grams

Protein: 2.5 grams
Fat: 9.5 grams
Calories: 143

Servings: 24
Prep time: 10 minutes
Bake time: 8 minutes

Based on a classic sugar cookie recipe, this type of cookie is a versatile treat to have with decaf tea or coffee. It also makes an excellent pie crust (see Rhubarb-Strawberry Pie, left).

½ cup almond flour

¾ cup Atkins Quick Quisine™ Bake Mix

1 cup granular sugar substitute

1 egg

1 egg yolk

1 teaspoon vanilla extract

4 tablespoons butter, softened

1 Heat oven to 350° F. In a bowl, whisk almond flour, bake mix, and sugar substitute. In a separate bowl, with an electric mixer on medium, beat egg and egg yolk, vanilla, and butter until well incorporated (mixture will not attain a smooth consistency). Beat in flour mixture just until combined.

2 Form dough into 24 small balls; arrange on a baking sheet 1 inch apart. Lightly flatten them with a fork to silver-dollar size. Bake 8 to 10 minutes, until set. Cool on baking sheets before transferring to a wire rack.

Atkins Tip: To make almond flour, process sliced or chopped blanched almonds in short, fast pulses, until a flour forms. Do not process beyond this point, as you'll end up with almond butter.

INDEX

CARBOHYDRATE GRAM COUNTER

FOOD ITEM	AMOUNT	CARB (G)	FIBER (G)	NET CARBS (G)	PROT (G)	FAT (G)	CALS
Milk, Cream, and Butter							
Butter	1 tbs	0	0	0	0.1	11.5	102
Half and half	1 tbs	0.5	0	0.5	0.5	1.5	20
Heavy whipping cream	1 tbs	0.4	0	0.4	0.3	5.5	51
Milk (whole)	1 cup	11.4	0	11.4	8	8.2	150
Milk (2%)	1 cup	11.7	0	11.7	8.1	4.7	121
Sour cream	2 tbs	1.2	0	1.2	0.9	6	62
Yogurt (whole milk, plain)	8 oz	11	0	11	9	8	150
Cheese							
American	1 slice	0.3	0	0.3	4.7	6.6	79
Blue, crumbled	2 tbs	0.4	0	0.4	3.6	4.9	60
Brie	1 oz	0.1	0	0.1	5.9	7.9	95
Cheddar	1 oz	0.4	0	0.4	7.1	9.4	114
Cottage cheese	1/2 cup	2.8	0	2.8	13.1	4.7	109
Cream cheese	2 tbs	0.8	0	0.8	2.2	10.1	101
Feta	1 oz	1.2	0	1.2	4	6	75
Mozzarella (whole milk)	1 oz	0.6	0	0.6	5.5	6.1	80
Parmesan, shredded	1 tbs	0.2	0	0.2	2.6	1.9	28
Ricotta (whole milk)	1/4 cup	1.9	0	1.9	6.9	8	107
Swiss	1 oz	1	0	1	8.1	7.8	107
Nuts and Seeds							
Almond butter	2 tbs	6.8	1.2	5.6	4.8	18.9	203
Almonds (whole)	2 tbs	3.3	2	1.3	3.8	9.1	103
Hazelnuts (whole)	2 tbs	2.8	1.6	1.2	2.5	10.3	106
Macadamia nuts, roasted	2 tbs	2.3	1.4	0.9	1.3	12.7	120
Peanut butter, natural, no sugar added	2 tbs	6.9	2.1	4.8	7.7	15.9	187
Peanuts	2 tbs	3.4	1.7	1.7	4.7	8.9	105
Pecans	2 tbs	1.9	1.3	0.6	1.2	9.7	93
Pine nuts	2 tbs	2.4	0.8	1.6	4.1	8.6	96
Pistachios	2 tbs	4.7	1.6	3.1	3.3	6.9	88
Pumpkin seeds	2 tbs	4.3	0.3	4	1.5	1.6	36
Walnuts	2 tbs	1.7	0.8	0.9	1.9	8.2	82
Grains, Breads, and Pasta							
Bagel, plain	3-1/2" diameter	37.9	1.6	36.3	7.5	1.1	195
Biscuit	2-1/2" diameter	26.8	0.9	25.9	4.2	9.8	212
Blueberry muffin	1 each	27.2	1.5	25.7	3.1	3.7	157
Corn flakes	1/2 cup	12.1	0.4	11.7	0.9	0.1	51
Corn muffin	1 each	28.9	1.9	27	3.4	4.8	173
Crackers, 100% stoned wheat	3 each	8.2	1.2	7	1.1	2.1	53
English muffin	1 each	26.2	1.5	24.7	4.4	1	134
Italian bread	1 oz slice	14.2	0.8	13.4	2.5	1	77
Oatmeal, plain (all cuts)	1/2 cup	12.6	2	10.6	3	1.2	73
Pasta, white, cooked	1/2 cup	19.8	0.9	18.9	3.3	0.5	99
Pasta, whole-wheat, cooked	1/2 cup	18.6	2	16.6	3.7	0.4	87
Pita, whole-wheat	6-1/2"diameter	35.2	4.7	30.5	6.3	1.7	170
Puffed rice cereal	1/2 cup	6.3	0.1	6.2	0.4	0	28
Raisin bran cereal	1/2 cup	23.6	4.1	19.5	2.8	0.7	93
Rice, white, cooked	1/2 cup	21.9	0.9	21	0.8	0.2	96
Tortilla, corn	1 small	12.1	1.4	10.7	1.5	0.6	58
White bread	1 slice	14	0.7	13.3	2.3	1	76
Whole-grain bread	1 slice	13.4	1.2	12.2	2.6	1.2	74
Soups							
Beef broth	8 oz	1	0	1	3	0	15
Bean w/bacon	8 oz	25	7	18	8	5	180
Chicken noodle	8 oz	8.7	0.8	7.9	3.3	1.9	64
Minestrone	8 oz	15	4	11	4	1.5	90
Tomato	8 oz	18	2	16	2	0	80
New England clam chowder	8 oz	13	1	12	4	2.5	90
Vegetable beef	8 oz	13	2	11	4	1.5	80
Condiments, Sauces, and Herbs							
Bacon bits	1 tbs	0.2	0	0.2	2.7	1.3	24
Chili powder	1 tsp	1.4	0.9	0.5	0.3	0.4	8
Cranberry sauce, whole or jellied	2 tbs	13.5	0.5	12.5	0	0	50
Dijon mustard	1 tsp	0.6	0.1	0.5	0.3	0.5	2
Fresh herbs, all types	1 tbs	0.1	0.1	0	0.1	0	1
Garlic	1 clove	1	0.1	0.9	0.2	0	4
Ginger root	1 tbs	0.9	0.1	0.8	0.1	0	4
Hollandaise sauce	2 tbs	1.7	0.1	1.6	0.6	2.5	30
Ketchup	1 tbs	4.2	0.2	4	0.2	0.1	16
Olives, black, large	5 each	1.4	0.7	0.7	0.2	2.4	25
Pesto sauce	2 tbs	2	0.9	1.2	5.6	14.2	155
Pickle relish	1 tbs	5.4	0.2	5.2	0.1	0.1	20
Salsa, red	2 tbs	2	0	2	0	0	10
Soy sauce/tamari	1 tbs	1	0.2	0.8	1.9	0	11
Marinara sauce	1/4 cup	6	1	5	1	0.5	30
Sweet & sour sauce	2 tbs	19	16	3	0	0.5	80
Tabasco® sauce	1 tsp	0	0	0	0.1	0	1

FOOD ITEM	AMOUNT	CARB (G)	FIBER (G)	NET CARBS (G)	PROT (G)	FAT (G)	CALS
Tartar sauce	2 tbs	4	0	4	0	10	100
White wine vinegar	1 tbs	0	0	0	0	0	5

Vegetables

FOOD ITEM	AMOUNT	CARB (G)	FIBER (G)	NET CARBS (G)	PROT (G)	FAT (G)	CALS
Artichoke	1 whole	13.4	6.5	6.9	4.2	0.2	60
Asparagus	4 spears	2.5	1	1.5	1.6	0.2	14
Green beans, steamed	1/2 cup	4.9	2	2.9	1.2	0.2	22
Broccoli flowerets, raw	1/2 cup	1.9	1.1	0.8	1.1	0.1	10
Cabbage, green, shredded, raw	1/2 cup	1.9	0.8	1.1	0.5	0.1	9
Carrot, 7.5" long, raw	1 each	7.3	2.2	5.1	0.7	0.1	31
Cauliflower, raw	1/2 cup	2.6	1.3	1.3	1	0.1	13
Celery, raw	1 stalk	1.5	0.7	0.8	0.3	0.1	6
Collards, steamed	1/2 cup	4.7	2.7	2	2	0.3	25
Corn, canned	1/2 cup	15.2	1.6	13.6	2.2	0.8	66
Cucumber slices	1/2 cup	1.4	0.4	1	0.4	0.1	7
Eggplant, broiled	1/2 cup	3.3	1.2	2.1	0.4	0.1	14
Endive	1/2 cup	1.8	1.4	0.4	0.4	0.1	8
Jicama, raw	1/2 cup	5.7	3.2	2.5	0.5	0.1	25
Kale, steamed	1/2 cup	3.4.	1.3	2.1	1.9	0.3	20
Lettuce, iceberg	1/2 cup	0.6	0.4	0.2	0.3	0.1	3
Lettuce, Romaine	1/2 cup	0.7	0.5	0.2	0.5	0.1	4
Mushrooms, portabello	4 oz	5.8	1.7	4.1	2.8	0.2	29
Okra, steamed	1/2 cup	5.8	2	3.8	1.5	0.1	26
Onions, chopped, raw	1/2 cup	6.9	1.4	5.5	0.9	0.1	30
Peas, frozen	1/2 cup	9.9	3.4	6.5	3.8	0.3	55
Peppers, green, raw	1/2 cup	4.8	1.3	3.5	0.7	0.1	20
Potato, baked, small	1/2 each	11.6	1.1	10.5	1.1	0.1	50
Pumpkin, canned	1/2 cup	9.2	5.1	4.1	2.1	0	41
Butternut squash, baked, cubed	1/2 cup	10.8	2.9	7.9	0.9	0.1	41
Tomato, small	1 (3 oz)	4.2	1	3.2	0.8	0.3	19
Zucchini, steamed	1/2 cup	2.6	1.1	1.5	1.1	0.1	13

Meat and Poultry

FOOD ITEM	AMOUNT	CARB (G)	FIBER (G)	NET CARBS (G)	PROT (G)	FAT (G)	CALS
Beef, prime rib	6 oz	0	0	0	37	56.4	667
Beef, salami	3 slices	1.9	0	1.9	10.4	14.3	181
Chicken breast, with skin, boneless	6 oz	0	0	0	50.7	13.2	335
Egg	1 each	0.6	0	0.6	6.3	5.3	78
Liver, calf	6 oz	10.4	0	10.4	40.5	9.9	304

Fish and Shellfish

FOOD ITEM	AMOUNT	CARB (G)	FIBER (G)	NET CARBS (G)	PROT (G)	FAT (G)	CALS
Salmon	6 oz	0	0	0	37.6	21	350
Clams, steamed	6 oz	8.7	0	8.7	43.5	3.3	252
Lobster, steamed	6 oz	2.2	0	2.2	34.9	1	167
Oysters	6 oz	6.7	0	6.7	12	4.2	117
Scallops	6 oz	4.9	0	4.9	34.7	6.7	228
Shrimp	6 oz	0	0	0	35.6	1.8	168
Squid, cooked	6 oz	6.4	0	6.4	32.2	8	236

Oils and Dressings

FOOD ITEM	AMOUNT	CARB (G)	FIBER (G)	NET CARBS (G)	PROT (G)	FAT (G)	CALS
Mayonnaise	1 tbs	0.1	0	0.1	0.2	11.2	100
Olive oil	1 tbs	0	0	0	0	13.5	119
Salad dressing, Caesar	2 tbs	1	0	1	1	16	150
Salad dressing, Italian	2 tbs	3	0	3	0	12	120
Salad dressing, ranch	2 tbs	1	0	1	1	18	170

Legumes (Beans)

FOOD ITEM	AMOUNT	CARB (G)	FIBER (G)	NET CARBS (G)	PROT (G)	FAT (G)	CALS
Baby lima beans	1/2 cup	21.2	7	14.2	7.3	0.4	115
Black beans	1/2 cup	20.4	7.5	12.9	7.6	0.5	114
Chickpeas/garbanzos	1/2 cup	20	7	13	5	2.5	120
Lentils	1/2 cup	19.9	7.8	12.1	8.9	0.4	115
Navy beans	1/2 cup	23.9	5.8	18.1	7.9	0.5	129
Pinto beans	1/2 cup	21.9	7.4	14.5	7	0.4	117
Soybeans	1/2 cup	10	3.8	6.2	11.1	5.8	127

Fruit and Fruit Juices

FOOD ITEM	AMOUNT	CARB (G)	FIBER (G)	NET CARBS (G)	PROT (G)	FAT (G)	CALS
Apple, medium	1/2 each	10.5	1.9	8.6	0.1	0.3	41
Applesauce, unsweetened	1/2 cup	13.8	1.5	12.3	0.2	0.1	52
Apricots, fresh, whole	3 each	11.7	2.5	9.2	1.5	0.4	50
Avocado, California (Haas)	1/2 each	6	4.2	1.6	1.8	15	153
Banana, small	1 each	23.7	2.4	21.3	1	0.5	93
Blueberries	1/2 cup	10.2	2	8.2	0.5	0.3	41
Cantaloupe	1/2 cup	7.4	0.7	6.7	0.8	0.3	31
Cherries	1/2 cup	9.7	1.3	8.4	0.7	0.6	42
Figs	1 small	7.7	1.3	6.4	0.3	0.1	30
Grapes, seedless	1/2 cup	14.2	0.8	13.4	0.5	0.5	57
Honeydew, cubed	1/2 cup	7.8	0.5	7.3	0.4	0.1	30
Kiwifruit	1 each	11.3	2.6	8.7	0.8	0.3	46
Lemon Juice	2 tbs	2.6	0.1	2.5	0.1	0	8
Mango	1/2 cup	14	1.5	12.5	0.4	0.2	54
Orange	1 each	16.3	3.4	12.9	1.4	0.1	64
Peach, small	1 each	8.8	1.6	7.2	0.6	0.1	34
Pineapple, fresh, chunks	1/2 cup	9.6	0.9	8.7	0.3	0.3	38
Plum, fresh, small	1 each	3.7	0.4	3.3	0.2	0.2	16
Raspberries, fresh	1/2 cup	7.1	4.2	2.9	0.6	0.3	30
Strawberries, fresh, whole	1/2 cup	5.1	1.7	3.4	0.4	0.3	22
Tangerine, small	1 each	7.8	1.6	6.2	0.4	0.1	31
Watermelon, balls	1/2 cup	5.5	0.4	5.1	0.5	0.3	25